A Life
That Really
Matters

Attention
UNITED METHODIST MEN

**This is the important story about what
happens when God's people**

get serious about their faith,
put God first in their lives, and
surrender themselves daily

**as they focus on God's plan and the
needs of others.**

This is a real story, lived by thousands of people and hundreds of congregations who have engaged the JOHN WESLEY GREAT EXPERIMENT since its birth in 1965.

Read about the story as Danny Morris—pastor of the church where it started—spiritual leader, and longtime friend and supporter of UNITED METHODIST MEN tells it. This book is a rewrite of the story told about the first group to use the "The Great Experiment."

Most importantly, we hope this book will cause YOU to bring the "experiment" to your men's group and your local church. We have refreshed the program with the release of a new journal book called

The Wesley Experience —*Surrendering to the Spirit*

The new journal replaces the booklet titled *The John Wesley Great Experiment,* authored by Sam Teague, and updated by The General Commission on United Methodist Men. The core of the original program has been retained, packaged in a contemporary journal format.

The new journal and EMS memberships are available by contacting
General Commission on United Methodist Men
P. O. Box 340006
Nashville, TN 37203-0006
Phone 615-340-7145 / Fax 615-340-1770

A Life That Really Matters

*The Story
of the
John Wesley
Great
Experiment*

Danny E. Morris

PROVIDENCE HOUSE PUBLISHERS
Franklin, Tennessee

First Edition 1965
Third Edition 1999

Printed in the United States of America

03   02   01   00   2   3   4   5

Library of Congress Catalog Card Number: 99-64723

ISBN: 1-57736-155-5

Cover design by Gary Bozeman

PROVIDENCE HOUSE PUBLISHERS
238 Seaboard Lane • Franklin, Tennessee 37067
800-321-5692
www.providencehouse.com

To Sam Teague

Contents

◆

Preface

◆

During the first thirteen years of my ministry I was a witness to a few (and far too few) personal conversion experiences. But during that time I never participated in an actual Pentecost. Until I finally did, I didn't know what I had missed.

The one who experiences a personal spiritual breakthrough is blessed by it during all of his days. One usually thinks of it as a pinnacle moment because it is life changing. The personal spiritual encounter actually requires the total Christian community—the church of which the person is a part—to validate the experience and to help the individual appropriate it.

But what I didn't know is that the Christian community, itself, has a separate and unique role to play in a spiritual breakthrough. The church itself is a primary receptor of special visitations of the Spirit of God. A personal spiritual encounter is coveted, but when a major spiritual breakthrough is experienced by a group of people it is even more phenomenal.

God's Spirit moving upon a person blesses the church. God's Spirit moving upon a group—large or small—not only blesses the church, it empowers the church for a new experience—a new level—of corporate spiritual vitality.

When it happens to an individual, we call it conversion. When it happens to a group, we call it Pentecost. My first Pentecost experience resulted from the John Wesley Great Experiment, "Wanted: Ten Brave Christians." I was not the prime mover. The Holy Spirit was. I did not have the leading role. Sam Teague did.

At the time, Sam was the highly dedicated, but thoroughly frustrated, teacher for our Christian Homebuilders' Sunday school class. In desperation he was moved to pray for the class. He prayed for about fifteen seconds and all *heaven* broke loose. The immediate visitation by the Holy Spirit within a period of twenty minutes after he prayed was a personal spiritual breakthrough that had within it the power of Pentecost. It still has that power after more than thirty years.

God answered that simple prayer in a profound way. The answer was recorded. The experiment was tried. A book was written. A spiritual movement was prompted.

I was there at the time. It happened in our group—first in one group then in several. The Pentecost power broke out in spiritual vitality at John Wesley Methodist (not United Methodist then) Church in Tallahassee, Florida. Since then, the challenge has spread widely and remains a remarkable ongoing catalyst for spiritual vitality.

There are some things I would love to know today:

1. How many persons have participated in the John Wesley Great Experiment?
2. How many churches have been impacted profoundly?
3. How many persons have entered the ministry of the church as a result of the Great Experiment?
4. How many marriages have found a spiritual center here?
5. How many pastors have recovered a sense of spirituality for ministry?
6. How many laypersons have been helped/changed/converted through their experience of the Holy Spirit in Great Experiment groups?

7. How many persons (including myself) have experienced the joy of tithing, and how many have never quit tithing?

I have too many more "how manys" to list them.

I regret that no data were kept and that stories were not systematically gathered. When it all began, how could we have known the impact the simple challenge would make? And if we had known, what could we have done about it?

There are some things we know:

- In excess of 200,000 copies of *A Life That Really Matters* have been published.
- Translations of the material have been published in six languages.
- The challenge has as much validity in the Philippines, India, and Australia as in Tallahassee, Florida.
- Small membership churches have an advantage with this challenge because it initially calls for a group of ten.
- Large membership churches have an advantage because multiple groups of ten to fourteen are manageable and some large churches have had two hundred or more to respond to the challenge at one time.

When someone asks me how the Great Experiment is doing, I say, "It continues to grind along somewhat like Coca-Cola," and it has continued to move forward for almost thirty-five years. Perhaps it is timely to tell the same story in today's language.

Hence, the rewrite of the original *A Life That Really Matters* while keeping the original title.

This text contains the profound story and challenge that was in the original book, but is updated with a new face to the future, in the belief that the invitation needs to be sounded again. The five spiritual disciplines are listed on the following page.

Wanted
Ten Brave Christians who will:

1. Meet once a week to learn how to pray.
2. Work at least two hours in the church each week.
3. Give God a tenth of one's earnings for the month.
4. Spend from 5:30 to 6:00 each morning in prayer and the study of Scripture.
5. Witness for God your experiences to others.

Many of us have a sense that this challenge is still valid:
• It is God's answer to a prayer.
• It may help you find some answers in your situation.
• It may be a timely invitation to your church.
Put God first and see what will happen!

A Word of Explanation

◆

This book is a rewrite of the original book, *A Life That Really Matters,* which told the story of how the program, the John Wesley Great Experiment, "Wanted: Ten Brave Christians," started and what happened to the first thirty-eight people who took part in it. The original story has carefully been retained in retelling. Most of this edition has been written anew with only a few of the original pages included.

There is a separate booklet, written by Sam Teague, entitled *The John Wesley Great Experiment.* It was published as a separate piece. It includes the "workbook" pages for the daily half-hour devotional period at 5:30 each morning. Twenty-one of those pages are noted for use in a "6:33 Club" for youth. (See the "6:33 Club" on page 78.)

We recommend that each participant have his or her own copy of *The John Wesley Great Experiment* booklet because it will become a spiritual journal as it is used during the month. It is essential that each person read *A Life That Really Matters* before committing to be in a group. There is more to the challenge than the five disciplines, and each person needs to comprehend the entire challenge before beginning.

We also strongly recommend that you do not water down this challenge:

- By making changes that will take the strength out of the disciplines;
- By doing only part of the experiment and anticipating maximum results;
- By making the challenge convenient for yourself or others; or
- By "pulling together" a group without the proper challenge for people to put God first!

Introduction

What's in a Name?

◆

The five spiritual disciplines of this experiment previously mentioned may be properly referred to by several names.

The Great Experiment
The John Wesley Great Experiment
The Brave Christian Program
"Wanted: Ten Brave Christians"

Any of the names are appropriate at various times and for several reasons.

The challenge is frequently referred to as the Great Experiment, for it is a *great experiment*! When a person undertakes to live these disciplines it is impossible to predict the power of impact or the eventual outcome, and so it is a great experiment. Also, the personal interactions of the particular people in a specific small group provide an experimental flavor to the process because every group is different.

Before the group tried this spiritual discipline in March, we were like a kindergarten scientist who had no idea what would happen if he put together two parts hydrogen and one part oxygen.

Instead of two, we made use of five "spiritual elements": prayer, service, tithing, Bible study, and Christian concern for others. What would happen when we used a catalyst, personal and total surrender to the will of God, we didn't know, and we never could have predicted what has happened.

Again, it is an experiment in that like a scientist we took known elements of the spiritual life and blended them in the crucible of our personal surrender to God. Until we *experienced this experiment*, we had no earthly way of knowing what would happen, for we had never "proved" the results.

But when one surrenders his or her life to God and practices a serious spiritual discipline, it ceases to be an "experiment" and miraculously becomes a "miracle."

A miracle! How else can you describe what happens when one is "born again, not of the flesh but of the spirit"? Even more miraculous than the blending of oil and water is the blending of the spiritual and physical into a unity dedicated, once and for all, to the will of God.

It is a miracle!

One month we were involved in a lot of *nothing*. The next month—through personal surrender to God and the practice of a spiritual discipline—we were involved in a *miracle*!

The John Wesley Great Experiment is also an appropriate name because the original challenge came in the John Wesley Methodist Church in Tallahassee, Florida

Wesley himself was a practitioner and advocate of the serious undertaking of personal and corporate spiritual disciplines. He was straightforward and to the point, as are these particular challenges.

It has also been referred to as the Brave Christian Program. Whatever the label, the program dimension is twofold. First, the challenge combines a variety of elements to make it a program: specific spiritual disciplines, a definite timeline, a small group culture, a particular lifestyle, a system of resources, a history, and a constituency. When all of these are combined, there is no doubt it is a program.

Secondly, numerous churches have developed a pattern of presenting this challenge at specific times of the year as a part of their ongoing effort of making disciples. A church in Texas found that combining a strong emphasis on evangelism explosion methodology and offering Great Experiment groups for all new members was a winning combination for new member commitment and assimilation. It became a major part of that church's program of spiritual renewal.

"Wanted: Ten Brave Christians" is a particularly powerful phrasing of the challenge phase of interpreting the emphasis and calling for response. Think of the number of members in your church. When the invitation is expressed as a call for "10" just 10 out of however many there are in your church, it is an ironic invitation. Out of 100 members or 540 members or 2,100 members or 4,000 members: *Are there even 10 who will put God first in these five simple ways for just one month?*

When the invitation is initially considered, one may quickly conclude that ten out of *this many* will be as easy as a snap of the finger.

Wanted: Ten Brave Christians. Are there ten; eight; how about four? Or will there be twenty-three? Or thirty-five? Do I hear fifty? How about seventy-five who will put God first in his or her lives in these specific ways? The question finally becomes personal: not how many, but will I be one?

This straightforward, disarming challenge has a way of becoming very personal. "If I am so sure we will find ten, why have I not decided to participate?"

Over a period of four to six weeks this challenge may be earnestly presented through a series of sermons interpreting the five disciplines. There is a great deal of homiletical content and direct teaching material for the series. Sunday school class interpretations and discussions augment the teaching quality of this period. A period of four to six weeks devoted to presenting the challenge will not be time wasted.

Chapter One

Always Fall . . . Reaching!

◆

"Always Fall . . . Reaching!" was not a song title until 1996. But it must have been the motto of countless persons across the centuries because it is a profound attitude that helps us make the most of our situations. If one *falls* . . . *reaching*, he or she is less concerned about *falling* than about *reaching*, about falling right, or protecting oneself in the fall. To fall . . . reaching is to hold on to your goal—even while falling; to be concerned with someone or something bigger than yourself. It connotes a remarkable disposition and effort, including sacrifice if it is needed.

Say hello to Sam Teague, a father of five, a banker, mayor of Florida's capital city, later elected state senator, a highly regarded speaker in his own church and other churches small and large, and also president for a time of the Florida Savings and Loan League, who on the morning of January 24, 1965, must have felt he was falling. He was unaccustomed to the feeling.

He had lots of good things going for him, but on that morning he would not have included on that list our Christian Homebuilders' Sunday school class, of which he was the teacher. He knew that it was not going well. The class members probably thought it was. They knew they were fortunate to have Sam as their regular teacher. He had defined "regular" as being their teacher for nine months, while being off duty from teaching during the summer.

After the first summer under this arrangement, the class discovered that he used those three months to carefully prepare an outline of subjects and content for his teaching. His lesson plans were always freelanced. He wrote his own teaching plans.

The class was delighted even if Sam was discouraged. They were actually giving their teacher an enthusiastic "hearing" each Sunday, but he felt that their response was less than it should be. They recognized that they had an outstanding teacher, and perhaps, they were being as "faithful" and supportive as they could be.

But for him, "listening to the gospel" and "actually hearing it" were not the same. They listened, but they didn't actually hear. That difference resulted in the frustration he was feeling on that Sunday morning. He had occasionally talked with me about how disappointed he was that even though his class members were bright, well educated, and stimulating, something was missing. For a long time he couldn't put his finger on it. Finally, it became clear to him. What was missing was their fervent response to the gospel. They loved the class, but the church didn't mean much to them. They would attend the class, be a wonderful, friendly, and likable group, but that was all. When the class ended each Sunday they would pick up their children and go home.

When he would vent his frustrations to me, my plan was always the same. I would hear him out, affirm his assessment, and encourage him to "go back into the game and give it your best." After all, teachers like Sam were hard to find.

His custom on Sunday was to go very early to his office in the bank and finalize his presentation for the class by preparing himself in a time of prayer and silence. So, on January 24, he had finished his period of final preparation for the class that day. After reviewing his teaching notes, he looked at the clock; 9:00, time to go. He put his things into his briefcase. Then it hit him!

He thought about the thirty-five or so young adults he would soon be speaking to and he said he felt empty inside—but not like he was hungry—a frustrated emptiness.

He thought, "Why am I doing this? What's the use? Nothing seems to get through to them. With so much potential, they are like plastic people in their understanding of the gospel." For weeks Sam had conducted a series about some of Jesus' strong words. He felt the class had no clue about what Jesus meant when he said, "You are light . . . You are salt . . . You are a city set upon a hill. Take my yoke upon you . . ." They just didn't have a clue.

Although he felt himself falling into utter frustration, he began reaching that morning. Reaching to God! Reaching to his students.

He leaned forward in his chair and put his head on the desk and reached out with a desperate, but brief prayer, "O God, show me how to challenge these young people so they can have a life that matters!"

Fifteen seconds max, if you pray it right!

Chapter Two

Putting God First

◆

"Show me how to challenge these young people so they can have a life that matters!"

Sam prayed in an effort to reach toward God and to reach for the class.

Since arriving at his office at about 6:50, he had prayed, sat in silence for awhile, and then had begun to concentrate on the simple survey he had asked his students to fill out on the previous Sunday. "Write the ten things that you want out of life in order of importance."

After tabulating thirty-three responses, he was shocked. The five or six most popular choices were *things*, material possessions such as: a new car, a second car, a house, a cottage at the coast, a boat, a different boat, financial security, more vacation time, extra money for vacation, and a vacation abroad.

Sam murmured to himself, "They think things will make them happy!" He was stunned!

At long last he had found a key—*they think the purpose of their lives is to be happy—and they think that the acquisition of things will make them happy*. It was clear from the survey that they desperately wanted to be happy because happiness was implied in most of the items they had listed. The shutter clicked and the picture was clear. Sam knew one can never find happiness by setting out to be happy. He knew that happiness is a byproduct, not an end in itself.

Jesus never talked about being *happy*. He was pretty strong and absolutely clear on "taking your cross," wearing "my yoke," going the second mile, giving to the poor, "dying and rising with me." None of this is happiness language. But when life is lived like this, happiness comes and is transformed into joy, and joy is real!

Later that morning Sam planned to tell his class about the results of the survey and had made a note to ask: "Why do you think you have a right to be happy? The purpose of your life is not to be happy but for your life to matter. If you set out to find happiness by itself, you will never find it. If you have a life that matters, happiness will come."

It was at this point in time that he looked at the clock on the wall, which read 9:00. Time to go!

With his notes placed inside, Sam snapped his briefcase closed, but before standing he looked off into the distance and reflected on the deeper implications of his discovery. With most of them under age thirty-five, he realized that with this attitude, they would have a lifetime of unhappiness while desperately trying to find happiness.

The weight of it was too much. While still seated, Sam almost tumbled forward to rest his head on the desk.

"God, show me how to challenge these young people so they can have a life that matters!"

It was a prayer, but there was no time for an "Amen."

Instantly, a thought came to Sam and he reached for a manila pad. A second thought almost overlapped the first. The ideas, thoughts, and concepts began to flow. He wrote rapidly, trying to capture everything. He flipped one page, then two. The avalanche of ideas continued. By the end of the third page, Sam was scribbling and using up more and more space to record fewer and fewer words and ideas.

The pace of his breathing increased as he began to sense a *presence* in the room. Although he was locked inside the bank, and his office door was closed, Sam felt he was no longer alone. There was a *presence!* It intensified as chill bumps developed on his arms. At one point, Sam actually turned to see if someone was standing behind him.

Looking back to the page, he had the sense that something was being written through his hand. It was a strange feeling, like he was not really connected to what was happening, but yet it was being done through him. Strange, but not frightening.

He kept rapidly writing and flipping page after page.

Finally, it stopped. It ended and there was nothing more to write. It was over. No more presence. No more thoughts and ideas. No more chill bumps.

With a deep exhale, Sam looked at the clock. It was 9:20. After praying a fifteen-second prayer, it had taken him twenty minutes to write God's answer. In that twenty minutes he had written the challenge of the Great Experiment, "Wanted: Ten Brave Christians," just as it had been given to him.

The challenge was to meet once a week to:

1. Learn how to pray.
2. Work at least two hours in the church each week.
3. Give God a tenth of one's earnings for that month.
4. Spend from 5:30 to 6:00 each morning in prayer and the study of the Scripture.
5. Witness for God one's experience to others.

This would be an experiment for one month. Putting God first during the month was the intention. Much more was written during the twenty minutes, but this was the heart of the challenge.

He quickly read over the pages he had scribbled and put in a few plainly lettered words where they were needed.

Sam then drove out to the church and proceeded as he had planned, but he didn't mention anything about the prayer or what followed it. He did say in two or three different ways that the purpose of life is not to be happy, but to have a life that matters. Not to be happy!

The Christian Homebuilder's class was stunned. Their cages had been rattled. A popular preconception had been challenged. As the class ended, the members were speechless.

On the way home, Sam recalled the name of the class and thought, "This morning we may have turned a corner in understanding how to build Christian homes. It has to do with putting God first in your life to the best of your ability, every day, in every way."

Chapter Three

Unless You Want To,
You Never Will

◆

Sam and I had been friends for a dozen years, fishing and hunting partners for several. While I was associate pastor at Trinity, where Sam and his family were active members, I discovered there was a need for a new Methodist church in Tallahassee. There had been an increase of twenty thousand in the area's population since a new Methodist church had been started.

On a fishing trip, we talked about this need. To my surprise he said, "If you will be the pastor of a new church, our family will become charter members. It will be tough to leave Trinity but we will change churches and stay as long as you stay. When you leave we will transfer back to Trinity." The executive director of the Tallahassee Chamber of Commerce later said he and Martha wanted to join the effort. So did Sam and Lurleen Murrow. All three families were upper vertebra backbone members of Trinity, key leaders in their church and the community. Within six weeks after the first Sunday, the new church had 144 charter members.

After starting the church, and over those first five years, Sam and I had grown even closer through church, hunting, and fishing. I frequently stopped by his office for coffee and conversation. I like to run around with bankers, senators, and mayors. Since he was the only one I knew, I stayed close by.

On the Monday morning following his fifteen-second prayer, we were awaiting our breakfast in the coffee shop next door to his office. Sam handed me a sheet of paper and said, "Take a look at this and tell me what you think."

I read, "Wanted: Ten Brave Christians," who for one month will put God first in the following ways:

1. Meet once a week to learn how to pray.
2. Work at least two hours in the church each week.
3. Give God a tenth of one's earnings for the month.
4. Spend from 5:30 to 6:00 each morning in prayer and the study of the Scripture.
5. Witness for God one's experience to others.

I said, "Where did you get this?"

"I'll tell you later. What do you think about it?"

I read the paper again.

"You aren't planning to do this in our church, are you?"

He kept pressing: "Tell me what you think."

As I took a deep breath I felt the blood leave my face. I realized I was severely threatened by what I was reading. We sat in silence until long after our breakfast came. I really appreciated the silence and I was glad Sam didn't press me further. I had all I could deal with in my sense of threat.

You see, I was the only pastor that church had ever had. I not only knew all of the nearly four hundred members, I knew them well. When I looked at those five challenges and thought about the people of our church, I was suddenly confronted with how weak and thin my spiritual leadership had been. My thoughts did not indict my church members, but myself. I had specialized in being a hale fellow, well met. This challenge was *spiritual stuff*, but my thing in the church was being optimistic, cheerful, fun loving—not spiritual. For five years I had preached a kind of synthetic "Norman Vincent Peale–ism," which would have made Dr. Peale sick in his midsection.

My feeling of threat was so great that I felt like striking out. I wanted to ask, "Do you think that many of our members will actually work in the church for two hours each week for a month?" I didn't actually ask the question because a hint of anger didn't seem appropriate right then. My anger had come quickly because of the fact that for a long time I had found it easier to do things myself than to try to talk half-interested people into doing something, and have to complete what they had half-done, or clean up their mess after them. Long ago, I had given up thinking it could ever be any other way. I had become cynical and weary. The emphasis on prayer, tithing, Bible study, doing something for someone else out of love—none of these had ever been my "thing" to preach about, to call for, or to expect.

By this point in time I could feel that I had a long face because I was becoming more and more uncomfortable. My feeling of being threatened went even deeper when I looked at the number ten. I thought, "I am the only pastor this church has ever had. If we can't find ten out of four hundred who will do this, how will it make me look?"

A few weeks later I was again reminded of how shallow my preaching and spiritual leadership had been and why I had felt so threatened that morning. I had decided to preach a series of Sunday night sermons for a calendar quarter. I was not in favor of services on Sunday night, but some of the members wanted this. After getting up for the morning service, it was hard for me to have much energy for another sermon so soon. This is why I began a series for the Sunday night services. The concept for the series seemed like a clever idea. I announced it: Thirteen sermons I love to preach. My plan was to review all of my sermons and select the best of the lot to preach (again) on Sunday nights. This would release me from sermon preparation since the sermons were already complete. It turned out to be a flawed plan. I had to terminate the series early because I couldn't find but five sermons I had the courage to repeat. During that sermon-hunting time I became appalled at the fluff I had been preaching. Think of how excited you would have been about hearing sermons with these titles: "Things

Never Are as Bad as They Seem," "Always Try to Be Optimistic," "It is Better to Be Healthy and Wealthy Than Sick and Poor," and "When the Whole World Seems to Be Crumbling at Your Feet—Keep Smiling!"

When I reviewed the last one in particular, I shuddered to think how the woman whose husband was dying with cancer made it through that sermon when all I had to say to her from the church was, "keep smiling!"

Is there any wonder I felt threatened that morning as I sat with my cup of coffee? My sense of threat came like a flash in my head. It felt like a brick had hit my stomach.

It was at about this point in my deep sense of frustration that the Holy Spirit began to minister to me. After looking up, and then back at the paper Sam had handed me, I began to think not of how our church was, but how it was intended to be. I remembered reading something Albert Einstein said, "The church in Germany was eventually the only force that stood squarely across Hitler's path to suppress the truth." (But we were not that kind of church!) Victor Hugo said, "The church is the anvil that has worn out many hammers." (But that was not us!)

I also thought of some things Jesus said, and immediately I realized that in a mystical way He was talking about our church: "You are the salt of the earth," "You are the light of the world," "You are my body in the world."

That is us! That may not be what we are right now, but that is what we are supposed to be—the body of Christ!

Suddenly, I wanted that to be true of our church. For the first time, I really wanted it!

I looked directly at my silent friend and felt courage growing in me. I leaned forward to say, "Let's see if we can find ten who will do these five things! If we can, it will blow the lid off our church. And if we can't, I will have something to preach about the rest of my life!"

I have only one way of approximating how long all of this took. When it was over and I could smile again, my untouched breakfast was still warm. But a major shift had taken place; a life change had come over me. I had discovered an entirely new orientation for a ministry of spirituality. I finally knew what the church was all about. It had come almost like a flash. And not a moment too soon!

That breakfast meeting was on January 24, 1965. Through the month of February we presented a robust challenge to "Put God First" in our lives. On March 1, we began the experiment. The lid did blow off our church. There were twenty-two in the prayer group in March and sixteen more in April. Spiritual vitality—even among a few people—does wonders for a church. Christ began to change people, to empower them, to set them free, to heal, give new life, to fill them with love. These things happened to almost everyone in the two groups and to some who were not in a group. You will read stories of some of them in subsequent chapters. After February and March of 1965, John Wesley Methodist Church was never the same again!

And I have had some wonderful things to preach about all these years since experiencing the miracle of a changed life. The following sentence gathers it all together for me and summarizes what I have been preaching about since 1965: "Unless you want to, you never will!"

Unless you want to
Put God First,
you never will!

Unless you want to
Live the Disciplined Spiritual Life,
you never will!

Unless you want to
Experiment with the Christian Faith,
you never will!

Unless you want to
Understand the Joy of Giving,
you never will!

Unless you want to
Release the Powerful Power of Powerful Laity,
you never will!

Unless you want to
Experience the Strength of Small Groups of People
Walking a Stretch with Each Other,
you never will!

Unless you want to
Discover the Power of Corporate Spiritual Discipline,
you never will!

These were possible for me! These are possible for you! These are possible for your church!

Undertake this thirty-day experiment and see for yourself. *Unless you want to, you never will!*

Chapter Four

Unpacking the Five Disciplines

◆

"Wanted: Ten Brave Christians" is an irony-laden, piercing probe that cannot be easily ignored by the congregation.

After a substantial effort to challenge the congregation by using "Wanted: Ten Brave Christians" as the flag of choice, let there be a response Sunday followed by a reasonable window of opportunity for persons to respond. The week following the response Sunday and the next Sunday will be ample time to gather the final responses and commence the groups.

When the groups begin, two adjustments are absolutely necessary: First, drop the terminology, "Wanted: Ten Brave Christians." (It can be picked up again for a later challenge period.) It should be dropped because this piercing probe of challenge has served its purpose. Those who are ready have responded. Those who did not respond should not be badgered.

Another reason to drop it is that no inference should be made that those who have responded have, thereby, become "Brave Christians." No terminology or label should suggest they have. Ironically, one does not become a "Brave Christian" because of joining one of these groups. That designation is only for one who makes a total surrender to God. What God asks of a person can never be done alone; only God can see him or her through. It is one's faith response in obedience and God working through the person that makes one a "Brave Christian."

Secondly, all of the groups immediately go underground. Within the church, hopefully, the challenge has been spirited, and the invitation has been forceful. The matter has been thoroughly talked about for quite awhile. When the groups begin, the *church will welcome a change* of subject because that will also mean a change in the forthright challenge to put God first.

Underground groups are also best because what occurs is kept within the groups through a strong code of confidentiality. Absolutely no effort is made to whet the interest of persons who did not respond.

Moreover, after the groups begin, it is inappropriate to refer to them as "Brave Christian Groups." They are only referred to as "Great Experiment Groups." List in the bulletin the *Tuesday Night Great Experiment* group meeting (date/time/location).

Several important factors make a good weekly meeting: Give due consideration to these segments in the meeting:

1. Prayer and learning to pray.
2. How the week has gone.
3. Devotional Bible study and discussion.
4. Hold all meetings at the same place each week. Do not serve refreshments.
5. Have the same convenor/guide for the month.
6. Remain focused on the subject of "Putting God First."
7. Have several spirituality books on the table at each meeting and invite everyone to peruse or read a book each week.
8. Stress the urgency of confidentiality. A good rule of thumb is that anyone may tell outside the group anything that happened to oneself, but should never tell outside the group what happened to another member.

We turn now to an inside look at the five disciplines. There are subtle rhythms even in the numbered order of the disciplines.

The first discipline is on prayer—an *inward* experience. The second is on service in the church—an *outward* experience. Tithing is an *inward* experience that is *outwardly* expressed. Silence, journaling, studying Scripture—*focuses on the day.* How to build and develop your life—*focuses on the future.*

The rhythms, therefore, become positive spiritual cross-currents within the small group setting. For all of its simplicity, the dynamics are present for the Great Experiment to make a dramatic impact upon the participants, and through them, upon the church and the world. When a church has multiple groups at the same time, and new groups are regularly being formed, they become a hotbed of spiritual ferment within the church.

Let us unpack each of the five disciplines to discover their uniqueness.

Discipline One
MEET ONCE A WEEK TO LEARN HOW TO PRAY

"Can I really learn how to pray?" is a top-rated question for many people. The question is usually closely held and is not often asked in public, but the question haunts many people.

The first discipline in the Great Experiment offers an emphatic "yes." Here is an index of group practices that fashions the answer to the question, "Can I learn to pray?" The answer becomes conclusive and convincing, "Yes, you can learn how to pray!"

Components of the Weekly Group Meeting:
  I. *The First Half Hour Is for Talking about Prayer and for Praying.*
  The weekly hour-and-a-half group meeting is specifically devoted to learning how to pray (and to two other important

matters). About one-third of the time is spent in talking about prayer and actually praying.

In the first month of our Great Experiment group we discovered it is important to put the half hour for prayer at the beginning of the meeting. Often the enthusiasm of the meeting will crowd out or use up the time allocated for the meeting and cause prayer to be curtailed. Prayer is too important to be left until last or to be shortchanged in its allotted time.

1. There is teaching and discussion about how to pray and there are a variety of types of prayer experiences.
2. Within the group, requests for prayer are freely called for and answers to prayer are carefully recorded.
3. Initially, persons are invited to pray silently. Later, the invitation will be given to pray voluntarily a sentence prayer. No one is ever forced to pray or to pray in a way that makes him/her feel uncomfortable.
4. The spirit and practices of prayer are positive and contagious.
5. Simple invitations and directions for prayer are varied.
   • Call for two minutes of silent prayer followed by the Lord's Prayer in unison. (Across the month, the time for silence may be lengthened.)
   • Invite anyone to say aloud a single word that expresses how one feels at the moment. (This is a simple form of prayer.)
   • Offer a prayer-word of thanksgiving to God.
   • Use a prayer-song, which the group may sing together. (Mallet's "Lord's Prayer" and others).
6. Invite persons to talk about meaningful times of prayer in their past, during the past week, today!
7. Associate these half-hour prayer-labs to the need for and possibilities of prayer in the coming week.
8. Suggest simple ways to pray in the coming week.

Although only one-third of the weekly meeting is about

prayer and learning how to pray, the entire hour-and-a-half meeting has the quality of a prayer group meeting.

II. *The Second Half Hour Is for Talking about How the Other Disciplines Went during the Past Week.*

    1. How have you done with the two hours working in the church?

Ask members to be specific. Is everyone caught up? Encourage them to not get behind in their schedule of service in and through the church.

    2. How have you done with the good deed?

Expect reports of success and failures. Ask for stories. This can be a rich time of realism, humor, honesty, confession, new resolves, etc.

    3. What have you learned about tithing?

How is it going? How do you feel about it? What are you learning about the use of your money and your relationship to God?

    4. How have you done with witnessing?

Many people have lots of confusion about witnessing. Simply put, witnessing is freely telling someone about something that happened to you. How to do that with grace and in good taste is a subject that can be helpful to a group of beginners. Within the group we discovered that witnessing is the most natural and comfortable thing a person does when something good has happened, and he/she is eager to tell someone about it. We also discovered that the reason some of us were negative about witnessing was that nothing especially good was happening or we had been negatively conditioned about witnessing, so we felt we had nothing to talk about.

III. *The Third Half Hour Is for Reflecting on the Daily Scripture Passages.*

Each morning at 5:30 assigned passage of Scripture of no more than nine verses is read, prayed about, and reflected upon in writing. This third half hour of the group meeting features each passage used at 5:30 each morning of the past week. It is a rich time of getting into the "Word" in a group, which may be very different from reflecting upon it alone.

It is Bible study, but the goal is not to do biblical criticism, nor is it a time for testing a person's orthodoxy. The purpose is to share the Scripture, devotionally.

Ideally, all seven passages that were read during the week are reviewed. Questions, comments, interpretations of meaning, and increased familiarity with Scripture are goals of this phase of the meeting.

Many people leave a Great Experiment group meeting with comments like: "Where have these passages been all of my life?" Or, "I didn't know that was in the Bible." Or, "The Bible is *something else*, isn't it?"

Discipline Two
WORK AT LEAST TWO HOURS
IN THE CHURCH EACH WEEK

"Unless we can do it in the spirit of love . . ." As pastor of the church, I have experienced many major discoveries about my sense of frustration and burnout. One discovery was that being a workaholic was not fulfilling. But I found it easier to "do it myself" than to try to find others who would follow through. At the time our Great Experiment started, I often felt like a basket case with everything I had to do. It caused anger in me. I had lived with it so long, I no longer knew the source of my negative feelings about my work.

When the Great Experiment started, I also discovered for the first time the power of a highly motivated and spiritually committed laity. It was a wonderful discovery, a lifesaver in pastoral ministry. In March we had twenty-two people who were doing 2 hours of service in the church each week for a total of 44 hours a week or 176 hours within the month. They continued serving 2 hours during the next month and were joined by sixteen more people. By the end of April (you do the math!) we had had 480 hours of work done in the church by both groups. By the middle of the first month my attitude had changed, and so had my problem!

My problem now was that we had run out of things for people to do. I dreaded to receive a call or have a visit by someone who wanted to "do their two hours" because I didn't know what to suggest. I learned something about highly committed and spiritually energized laypeople: You can ask them to "hold up this wall" and they will do it for awhile, but they are sharp! Before long they will figure out that the wall will stand up without holding it. I am saying that I couldn't just give them "busy work." They were serious about living out their faith and the work had to have meaning. By the middle of March we were beginning to run out of things to do. All of the prospects and shut-ins had been visited; people in the hospitals were being systematically visited by our laity for the first time; the flower beds were in great shape; the choir was full; we had one Sunday school teacher for every eight children; and the classrooms had been painted. Within eight minutes after the call went out at a meeting one evening, we had all of the vacation church school teachers and helpers we needed for an expanded program, and on, and on, and on!

And my attitude: within far less than two months I found new hope for the church. Those dry bones were alive for the first time.

Our laity's eagerness to respond was carefully honored and managed. At the first meeting of the month we presented a list of things that needed to be done in the life of the church. Here is the list we prepared:

A Beginning List
Please read over this beginning list of opportunities for service and choose the items that will challenge you most.

1. Visit hospital patients or shut-ins, representing the church.
2. Visit present members to tell them about your experience in the Great Experiment.
3. Visit families interested in our church and invite them to join. (Names will be provided by the church secretary.)
4. Be a teacher or helper in a Sunday school class for a month. (One hour for preparation as helper and one hour for class time.)
5. Join the choir for a month. (Count as one hour per week.)
6. Visit in your neighborhood for one or two hours to find "prospects" for the church. Invite them and report prospects to the pastor.
7. Within your neighborhood, spend an hour visiting two or three church families whom you do not know to get acquainted and to talk about our church and its needs—spiritual and physical.
8. Visit with some new members to get acquainted, to welcome them, to tell them of your experience. Perhaps two or three can be visited in an hour. (The pastor will furnish names.)
9. Help provide Sunday school room improvements. (The trustees will guide you.)
10. Be a telephone person (one hour per week). Names will be provided through the church office.
11. Work out details for, and promote the formation of, a church library during the month.
12. Work in the church office (one or two hours).
13. Work on the church grounds—a continuing need.
14. Contact visitors from the previous Sunday in their homes.
15. Use your imagination to discover other things the church needs you to do.

We asked everyone to select an item and put his or her name by it so needed coordination could be done, so overlaps could be spotted, and so gaps could be covered. These were accountability sheets, not for reprimanding anyone, but to underscore the urgency of the commitment. The list also reflected the strength of our corporate efforts.

We encouraged everyone to strive to put in their two hours week-by-week instead of saving up for one big day at the end of the month. One can fulfill the "letter of the commitment" that way, but the spirit of ongoing service to God would be missed.

There is no way to overstate the spiritual and physical revolution within our church experience through this simple discipline of a few people working at least two hours in the church each week.

The revolution was not just in the work that was done, nor in the number of people involved, nor in the number of hours that were tallied up, nor in the enthusiasm that was evident. The revolution went far deeper.

Everything was being done in the spirit of love.

Love for God,
Love for the Church,
Love for each other as sisters and brothers in Christ,
Love was the key.

The change in just one month was hard for me to comprehend.

In March this was the same church that was here in February. These were the same people. The same jobs. *But everything was different!*

I no longer had reasons for negative feelings about the response of these persons. Nor did I have to prod, or "clean up" when they finished. They became self-starters, initiators, and innovators. I was shocked at the change from one month to the next.

"Unless we can do it in a spirit of love. . . ." The following taglines became some of our favorite ways to complete the previous sentence.

Unless we can do it in a spirit of love . . .

we will not do it!
it is not worth doing!
count me out!
forget it!
it does not belong in the church!

As a church we had made two of our greatest discoveries: (1) everything that is done in the church must be done in the spirit of love; and (2) the church needs nothing done in its life that cannot be done in the spirit of love—*nothing*!

Suddenly, we had two new North Stars to guide us as a church.

Discipline Three
GIVE GOD A TENTH OF ONE'S EARNINGS FOR THE MONTH

"Giving until it helps" became a goal of our church.

It was surprising to me to learn that the challenge of tithing for a month was one of the disciplines of the Great Experiment. I had not learned much from being a tither for more than a dozen years, so I wondered what could be learned about tithing in just a month.

The reason I had been tithing all of my adult life was that I knew I was supposed to promote tithing and, therefore, I needed to be doing it if I expected others to do it.

I had tithed all that time *and hated every minute of it*! I had missed the significance of tithing in two ways: (1) I had a poor motivation for doing it; and (2) I had done it the wrong way.

When Sam began advocating tithing in his class he suggested a different way of doing it.

First, he made it clear that the reason for tithing was to put God first. I had never understood that before. I saw tithing as an official requirement of my job as a pastor, which made it feel like legalism.

Second, he invited (taught) us to take the tithe out first: "Let your tithe be the first check you write when you get paid. *Put God first* in spending your money."

What he said seemed so right. He didn't get my attention because he was a banker—although that fact was refreshing—it sounded right from a faith point of view.

I had been doing exactly the opposite of what he was suggesting; I had always given my tithe last, after everything else had been paid—and when I was about to, or had already, run out of money. I was doing it legalistically, so I put it off as long as I could, and ended up giving begrudgingly most of the time. The result was that I was giving to God when I had the least to give. I was giving out of my poverty. No wonder it was a continuing chore.

But in the Great Experiment, we were taught to give our tithe first. When we had the most to give—to give out of our abundance.

What a difference even one month of tithing this way made for my wife, Rosalie, and me. Tithing suddenly became a joy and a religious experience, but not just because we were tithing. It became that way because we were now *putting God first* in the very important matter of our money. But there was more to learn.

The third thing Sam suggested was that we pray about how we spend the other 9/10. Rosalie and I had never prayed about how we spent our money. (The closest we had come was praying because we needed more money.)

If taking the tithe out first sounded right, praying about how we spent the other 9/10 sounded absolutely necessary. We were struggling to live off of 10/10 and sometimes 11/10 or 12/10. How could we manage on only 9/10? Prayer was absolutely necessary! It would take God to help us pull it off.

Remember, some of the things we regularly talked about at our weekly meetings were prayer, tithing, how it was going with us, etc. As we talked in our group, we discovered we were all "in the same boat." Before we began tithing, none of us felt that even 10/10 was enough for our needs.

The stories began to accumulate. We heard over and over that since beginning to tithe in these ways, money seemed to go further. Nine-tenths became as much or more than 10/10 had been. The difference was not because anyone received a raise, nor because there was *magic* in prayer. Rather, we discovered there was *power* in prayer. Money had suddenly taken on new meaning. Can you believe that money had become a spiritual matter? That is precisely what happened! Money became supremely important and we began to spend our money prayerfully. That helped us to spend it more wisely. The result was that we were actually spending less. All of these discoveries were startling for everyone in the group.

One of our most memorable tithing stories was shared at our first meeting. Marilyn and Calvin were a young couple, struggling over whether to be in our first group. Sam and I had announced on Sunday that anyone would be in the group who signed up that Sunday or mailed in their commitment form that was postmarked before midnight on Monday. Thereafter, the group would be closed for the month. Calvin had gone home for lunch on Monday, and he and Marilyn had one final discussion over the last point of their struggle: *Could they give a tenth of their income for the month*? They figured the dollar amount and decided to take a step of faith. They signed the commitment and sealed the stamped envelope just as they heard the postman coming.

Marilyn quickly flipped through the mail before Calvin left for work and noticed an unusual envelope. She opened it and found a letter from a man who had owed them money for a couple of years. Long ago they had concluded he would never repay them. The man had written to apologize for the delay in paying and had included a check.

The check was for the exact amount of the monthly tithe they had just computed before signing their commitment form.

At this point in their story they were both in tears of awe and joy, as were many in our group.

Calvin told us something we would all come to experience: "We may find it is hard to outgive God!"

Discipline Four
SPEND FROM 5:30 TO 6:00 EACH MORNING IN PRAYER AND MEDITATION

Where has the Bible been all of my life?

The early morning time of prayer and meditation quickly gave rise to this question. That half hour is a powerful part of this challenge. One reason is the uniqueness of three ten-minute segments of the devotional period. *In the first ten minutes read a different passage of Scripture each day, pray about its meaning, and write in less than fifty words and in less than ten minutes what the passage says to you.*

During a six-week period, Sam surveyed three hundred passages with a concordance and selected thirty-one. No passage had more than nine verses. He carefully arranged them in a wavelike pattern so that they had a rhythmic strength of impact. Many people have commented that the subsequent three months of selected passages are devoid of the strength of this rhythm. I suppose that is so because he selected them under spiritual inspiration.

During the second ten minutes, pray about one good deed you will do for one person that day. Name the person, name the good deed, and write these in the notebook. (At first I thought that was lots of bookkeeping, and it is, but the bookkeeping is the easy part.)

These two ten-minute devotional exercises provided an interesting contrast. In the first ten minutes, the focus is on the "oughtnesses of God." "You are the salt of the earth." "You are the light of the world." At least, according to Scripture, that is the way you ought to be!

In the second ten minutes, the focus is on "the good deed," which reflects how it really is with you.

This contrast was very revealing, even on my first day. I did O.K. with the first ten minutes and was able to move right into the scriptural "oughtness" for that day. But when I moved on to the second ten minutes to think about a good deed, I ran out of time because ten minutes was not enough. Since we had been told of the value of disciplining ourselves not to tarry, but to move on in the pattern of the three ten-minute segments— it being so early in the morning with the natural tendency to be overcome with sleepiness—I moved beyond the second ten minutes to the exercise of the final ten minutes. I planned to later return to my effort to decide on a good deed. When I finished and returned to the second ten-minute exercise, I continued to be stumped on naming a good deed.

Every good deed I thought of would not hold up under the guidelines that had been suggested: "Select a good deed you will not get paid to do or you are not obligated to do." Visiting someone in the hospital might qualify as a legitimate good deed for others but not for me. I was getting paid and was obligated to visit people in the hospital.

Even—and maybe especially—Brother Tom "paid" me when he would say, "Danny, seeing you just makes my day and gives me such a lift." Pretty good pay! No one else told me that. Hearing something like that made it worthwhile to go out to the hospital. I began to evaluate my motive for the things I was doing—"for others."

On the previous day I would have honestly said that maybe 75 to 80 percent of my deeds for others were done unselfishly. But hear this: Why did it eventually take me one hour and forty minutes that day to think of one unselfish thing I could do for just one person in an entire day?

I was at first chagrined and then devastated by how self-centered and self-serving I was. Devastated!

After eventually finishing the three segments that were supposed to be ten minutes, I was just sitting there. I noticed that both of my elbows were resting on the arms of my chair. It seemed a natural alignment to cause my fists to rest against each other, knuckles touching. I began to rotate one fist one way and one the other. This simple action dramatized what I was feeling and the disharmony I had discovered about myself. How it "ought" to be, and how it "really was" with me were not in sync. That was a tough discovery.

With this shattering contrast of disharmony in my life before me, I reconsidered what I had written earlier when I had jumped ahead to the assignment for the third ten minutes. I read my answer to the question, "How do you want to build and develop your life?" I could now see it clearly. What I had written was pitiful, flimsy, shallow, and out of focus.

I put my fists back together, knuckles touching, and rotated them again as before to be reminded of the disharmony within my life. Suddenly, there was no mystery about why I was feeling that my life was not together, why I was feeling fractured. I was out of sync with God's plan for me. The evidence was right there in what I had just written about building and developing my life.

I began rotating my fists back and forth with my wrists turning together in the same direction. That was an image of the harmony I wanted in my life. I could see clearly what was needed. Now I could really answer the question, "How do you want to build and develop your life?" (Just one thought per day will be excellent progress.) That question now had meaning. I scratched through what I had just written, so I could write something else. But I didn't stop with just one thought. I wrote and wrote in my daily journal as insights flooded my mind. This dynamic rhythm of God's oughtness, my response (reflected in struggling with the good deed), and insight about building and developing my life, had walloped me the very first day. I was not the only one who would experience this powerful rhythm.

On about the third day in our group a man answered the question about building and developing his life. "I want to be a millionaire!" he said. He was already well on his way to attaining his goal. Toward the end of the month he wrote in the margin of that page: "This goal is not good enough for a child of God!"

Observations about the three ten-minute practices of meditation:

• This is a wonderfully simple structure for a devotional period.

• It is simple enough for the beginner and challenging enough to be beneficial for anyone.

• It serves as a *reality check* for everyone who will stand in the crosscurrents of these three movements for thirty (or thirty-one) days.

• To top it off, the person meets weekly for discussion—for confirmation or confession—with others who are doing the same devotional discipline.

• This half hour, early morning, daily devotional period is a remarkable experience.

Discipline Five
WITNESS FOR GOD YOUR EXPERIENCES TO OTHERS

"What is so wonderful about a Christian witness?" (And what is so frightening about it?)

Of all the disciplines, witnessing was probably the most challenging. Some would even say it was the most frightening. A few people later said they decided not to participate in the Great Experiment because of the call to witness. Previously they had been turned off by stereotypes of people standing on the street corner passing out tracts, or by street preachers, or by having been accosted by someone about religion.

That was not the type of witnessing being advocated. We talked a lot about how natural witnessing is and how simply it can be done. Many examples came forth through our willingness to *experiment* with witnessing. Some of our efforts were successful and some were not. We learned from each other, and we "practiced" witnessing within the group by telling each other when something that was being said or done was negative or did not communicate.

Surrender in the Christian Life
by Nelda Drymon

Nelda Drymon, a mother with a twelve-year-old son read us her witness at one of our meetings. She came to our church just as the Great Experiment was beginning and joined the first group. Through her written witness she had captured a vital insight about the importance of surrender in the Christian life.

All my life my father taught me to love the Scripture. When I was growing up prayer was always a part of our home. Prayer and Bible reading have been a continuing practice of my life since I was a little girl. I can't remember when I was not a Christian.

All of this time I have thought that being a Christian meant giving up something. But on the very first day I went to the Christian Home Builders' class, I heard Mr. Teague talk about surrendering our lives to God. The more I thought about the word *surrender*, the more concerned I became. I didn't know how to surrender my life to God any more than I already had.

I had been a Christian all of my life. I had not only read, but had studied the scriptures—I have read the Bible through many times. I had experienced the presence of God in my life; I had depended upon God all of my life.

But that word *surrender* kept coming back to my mind. How could I really *surrender* my life to God more than I had?

It was on Sunday afternoon, March 14, that I found my answer. I was doing some things around the house, but my mind was constantly on the matter of "surrender." I kept asking "how"? In an attitude of prayer, I kept asking this question over and over again!

And suddenly, the thoughts began to come so rapidly I could not write them in full. But I managed to jot down some bits of my thoughts that meant so much to me.

As I thought of the word *surrender* it brought to my mind, of all things, a time of war between two countries. When one side loses, their first action is to surrender to their victors. This point of surrender has not been reached without a fight and it is not a happy time. But the surrender is complete—their men, their equipment, their land, and most of all, their pride and independence. I thought of the struggle I have been having in my own soul.

As I considered this, suddenly, I realized that this is exactly what God expects me to do—surrender all that I am; my life, my service, my pride, and my independence. My surrender must be complete!

Again I thought of the two countries. On the side that surrenders there are good men, equipment, and land. There are average men, equipment, and land. And along with these, poor and very poor men, land, and equipment.

The victor will accept all of these categories and work with each. The good will strengthen into the best. Average will be motivated to better. Poor will be given an opportunity to respond. And even the very poor will be given the opportunity. But if that which is very poor makes no response, the victor will give attention to the others.

At this point I thought, "I can 'give up' the poor and very poor habits in my life, but this takes me no further because when I 'give up' something, I give them to no one."

On the other hand, when I surrender my life to God I surrender the good, the average, the poor, and the poorest. And God will work with each category, God can decide—and help me to decide—what in my life needs to be cast off.

God is the Victor, so to speak, and will raise each category or cast aside those things which are unimportant and unworthy.

This was a new thought for me and because of it I made a new commitment. I surrendered my life to God, and God accepted me as I was—my good, my average, my poor, and my poorest. God will teach me through the Word, through prayer, and through my service to God and to others, what matters in my life and how to live in God's will. This is what it means to me to surrender my life to God!

Chapter 5 is about *witnessing*—what it is and is not; what we discovered about it; how we began to do it; and some witnesses of several people from across the years.

Chapter Five

The Witness of the People

◆

What is so wonderful about a Christian witness?

There are many factors that make a Christian witness powerful and one of the most essential forms of communication the church has ever produced:

Simplicity   The truth it reveals
Authenticity   Mystery
Clarity   Surprise
Passion   Necessity
The story it tells

In short, there is nothing that can take the place of a vital and alive personal Christian witness. The church thrives on it and is strengthened and thrilled by it. The church is hungry for it and wants to hear it, to foster it, and to insure that it continues. When someone gives her Christian witness, either in what she says or in what she does, it produces gladness, goodness, and hope to all who hear it or see it.

When we began to take personal witnessing seriously in our group, everyone was timid and cautious. We had seldom (or never) witnessed and we were unsure, or even fearful.

Early in our group's experience of witnessing we read what R. L. Johnson of Albany, Georgia, had said in giving his personal witness. His witness was in the form of a challenge, which grew out of his participation in the Great Experiment.

I will challenge any man or woman to sit quietly in prayer and meditation at 5:30 A.M. for thirty days and then tell me that he prays but his prayers have no meaning.

I will challenge any man or woman to plan a totally unexpected and unselfish deed daily for thirty days and then tell me she does not love her fellowman.

I will challenge any man or woman to set to writing bit by bit over a period of thirty days at 5:30 A.M., what he expects to make of his life and then tell me he has made no effort to conform to the written design.

I will challenge anyone to perform the three above functions and then say he/she does not enjoy sharing his experience with others.

Here are examples that illustrate some of the values of witnessing which we began to discover in our group. These seem to fit naturally within the five disciplines of the Great Experiment.

Discipline One at Work
MEET ONCE A WEEK AND LEARN HOW TO PRAY

New Birth Through Prayer
Danny E. Morris

About a week before I assisted with Merle Jackson's funeral last month, she wrote me a long letter reviewing her story she had shared with me. Early on in the letter she stated that she didn't know how her story would be beneficial to anyone else, but she was glad to share it if it might.

I thought back to how she and I had clicked with each other years ago when she visited our church and how warmly I was received in my first visit in her home. From then on, we liked each other.

She began attending our church regularly, and on my next visit to her home, she told me of the hurt and anguish of her childhood years. Her father was a hard and insensitive man. Her stepmother resented her and was a hateful person. Even the stepmother and Merle's father didn't get along well together. She said she had felt no love as a child, and she had no self-esteem as a teenager or when she became an adult. She did not go to church regularly while growing up, and when she did, it was usually unwillingly, because she felt that God could not love someone like her. Tears flowed freely as she spoke.

On that visit we touched at an even deeper level than we had earlier. Before leaving that day I prayed that her father and stepmother would be forgiven, that Merle's hurt and memory would be healed, and that she would be able to accept God's love.

In the next few weeks I began to notice a change in her countenance. Instead of looking sad, she began to shift more easily back and forth between a broad smile and a pleasant look. She had begun to have what I often think of as someone with a recently, freshly washed face. That was something new for her.

In her letter last month she recounted a spring afternoon about twenty-eight years ago. She and her husband, Jack, were sitting on the patio. Suddenly, she looked at her watch, jumped up, and hurried away saying, "Jack, don't worry about me, I am going to the church." She described how panicked she felt when she realized that the first Great Experiment group in our church was starting at 7:00 P.M. The time had slipped up on her; it was already 7:10. She drove wildly, by her own description, not fully stopping for two stop signs. From the parked car she ran to the front of the church and suddenly froze in her steps.

She looked at the flowerpot beside the steps and the clump of daffodils that were "blooming their hearts out," as she put it. She had never before noticed the flowerpot, but *she had seen those daffodils*—in a wonderful dream two nights before. There was no doubt; it was the same bunch of daffodils. She stood absolutely still trying to put together her dream, the flowers which she was seeing now for the second time, and her utter excitement of finally being at the church—even if a little late.

She wrote about that moment: I hesitated in the narthex because I could hear you speaking to the group. The meeting had already begun. My heart sank. How could I walk in late? But I had to do it! I took a deep breath and pushed open the door. You looked my way and said, "Oh, Merle. We've been waiting for you. Welcome home!" And I timidly entered and sat down.

Danny, I knew that you had spoken those words and that you were just being hospitable. But to me, it was as if those words were spoken to me by God: *Merle, we've been waiting for you. Welcome home!* As I sat down, tears were flowing down my face. I sat there trembling, weeping, *coming home*, feeling for the first time that God really loved me! I listened to everything you said that day with a great sense of awe. I couldn't wait for the first day to begin our Great Experiment. Oh! It was *something!* Prayer . . . the group . . . discussing scripture . . . talking about our good deeds each day . . . laughing a lot—and all the while, being spiritually born anew. I mean, *totally, new birth!*

Danny, I am in my early seventies, but my life actually began only twenty-eight years ago when we had our first Great Experiment group at the church. Do you understand what I am saying? That is when my life began. I was *born* just twenty-eight years ago!

As I read her letter, I thought about the telephone call I received from Merle on my birthday more than twenty years ago. She always sent me a birthday card, with a poem she had written, and usually a letter. But when she called that day she gave me the greatest birthday gift I have ever received. She briefly reviewed these facts of her journey and said, "Danny, you led me into a totally new life, in Christ. I began to live for the first time while you were here. You will never know what you mean to me."

Her generous accolades made me feel uncomfortable, so I interrupted by saying, "Thank you, Merle. It is so kind of you to say those things."

Then came her gift to me. She said, "Danny, there has never been a day since Christ came into my life that I have failed to pray for you by name. I have never missed a day praying for you!"

I was stunned!

I said, "Merle . . . I am so moved to hear you say that! My word . . . what a gift to give me on my birthday—the greatest gift I could ever receive. Merle . . . thank you!" That was twenty years ago.

When I got near the end of the letter, written a month before she died, she said again, "Danny, I have prayed for you by name every day since I was converted twenty-eight years ago."

In the Great Experiment, the first thing Merle committed to do was to "learn how to pray." I was the beneficiary of her learning to pray. As I have reflected on her gift, I have concluded that Merle's faithfulness in prayer and her continuing love for me have been shaping influences upon my life and ministry.

As we flew to Florida for her funeral last month, I was thinking how fortunate I was to have been the one Merle selected to pray for by name every day. At her funeral, I told about her call on my birthday and what it had meant to me across the years. I could not keep back my tears as I spoke about it.

After the service, four people came to me and said that Merle had also prayed for them every day by name for years! *I wonder how many more there are whose names she regularly called in prayer.*

When the fourth person came to me to say that Merle had prayed for her, I said, "Isn't that just like her? And all this time I thought I was special!" We laughed, and my friend said, "All of us were special to Merle."

I think it is fair to say that no matter what else she got out of the Great Experiment, Merle *learned how to pray.*

The "Happy" Experience
Happy Woodham

The Reverend Ben C. Johnson of the Lay Witness Mission Movement, in speaking to the Layman's Conference of the Southeastern Jurisdiction, told of his visit to a prayer group meeting.

For three months, I had heard of the work of the Holy Spirit that was underway at the John Wesley Church . . . how I wanted to talk with these folks who had been in the stream of the Spirit. Finally, a time came when I could visit. Danny Morris, whom I had just met at a communications workshop at Emory, filled me with expectancy.

Brother Sam and his wife Myra entertained us at the Capitol City Country Club with a delightful sirloin—amazing how easy it is to talk over the aroma of a good steak.

After dinner, we hastened on to one of the branch banks. In the conference room there were a dozen people assembled. They were surprised to see us. But our excitement was far greater than their surprise, because we had heard just enough at supper to double our interest.

I asked Sam to let me simply be a listener. He graciously consented by not calling on me to say anything about my own particular interests. One by one I listened to living witnesses of Jesus Christ.

One man sitting just across from me worked in the grocery business. With a radiant beam in his eye, he began describing what Jesus Christ had done for him. His life had been dull and uninteresting; he long since had asked that all-important question, "What is life all about?" Yet for a long time he was filled with frustration because he had received no answer. I got more excited as he told how the program of the "Ten Brave Christians" had challenged his life and given him a new direction and the answer to his question.

While this man was sharing, I kept noticing out of the corner of my eye a slightly built man sitting two seats from me. All the time the others were talking he kept switching from hip to hip as though he could not sit still. He smiled . . . he twisted his hands . . . he looked at the group . . . and twisted some more! Like a three-year-old at Churchill Downs on Derby Day, he kept standing in the shoot ready to run. "What did he have to say?" I wondered.

A lady shared. She had been the victim of alcohol for several years and now she had found in Christ the answer to her inner frustration. Christ had made her a whole person. This was no negative fanatic; she just did not need alcohol any longer.

Finally, we got to the next man, the man who couldn't sit still. His name was "Happy." I never learned more than that; I suppose that was enough. Happy began his story:

"This is the greatest thing in the world, this brave Christian deal." As he talked, his countenance glowed with mingled joy, love, and excitement. He was contagious!

"I will tell you what this spiritual discipline has done for me"—all the time he was switching hips, twisting his hands, and making a few amusing faces—"it has changed my life."

He went on to tell about several things that had long been deep problems for him, and his recent victory over them.

"Right now," he said, "both of my partners are out of town and the business is as rushed as it can be. Now, when I was nervous," he uttered—between a gesture, a jolt, and a jerk—I secretly smiled to myself. "When I was nervous I would have climbed the wall under such pressure. Now, I just go in the back room and look up, asking, 'Lord, what will we do?' And He gives me the answer."

Happy's own joyous, jovial spirit would have been witness enough; his worded expression added something else. Then he said, "You know the Lord has a sense of humor too," and he related an experience.

"The other night while I was having my evening prayer time, I really made contact, got plugged in . . . you know! It was a wonderful time. But when I finished and crawled into bed, I got scared nearly to death. The room had been completely dark for quite awhile. I casually opened my eyes and began to see lights flashing on and off. One here, one there. Everywhere I looked there were little lights all in the room flashing on and off . . . on and off!

"I sat up in bed and whispered to my wife, 'Rose, Rose wake up! Rose, wake up, I'm about to have a vision.' I hadn't been a Christian but three months and here I was having a vision already!

"Then Rose sat up. She looked about, hopeful to share in my vision. For an instant she, too, was stunned by what she saw. "I whispered, 'I don't know anything about visions! Can you make out any meaning to it?'

"Then Rose exclaimed, 'Happy you aren't having a vision . . . those are lightening bugs that got out of little Peggy's fruit jar!'"

I agree with Happy, "The Lord does have a sense of humor!"

God Is Love
Joanne Surles

Joanne is a housewife in her early thirties and the mother of two children; she is also a charter member of the church.

I have been looking for something all my life, but I looked in all the wrong places. Although I was brought up in the church, I never seemed to reach anything spiritual there. As I grew older, church became a social thing. About the only time I was ever touched in church was by an occasional favorite old song. But even then the good feeling I received was just a short-lived emotion.

As I grew older, I began to do the things the church had always warned me not to do. They never explained exactly why I should not drink, and it gave me an hour or two of peace-of-mind, so why shouldn't I drink? I became guilt ridden as I did the things I had been taught not to do, but because I could think of no "valid reason" not to do them, I continued to live as I pleased. In doing so I became nervous, irritable, and cynical. I began having headaches, an upset stomach (the beginning of an ulcer), and many other aches and pains too numerous to mention.

It is hard to explain to anyone who has never been completely cynical about God just how unhappy a person can become. I would sometimes sit up in bed in the middle of the night in a cold sweat, wondering what was to become of me. I prayed, but never really expected my prayers to be answered, and they never were! Because I am a normally intelligent person (I think), I wondered a lot about life after death, why we are here, etc., but the answers always seemed to be just around the corner. I talked to probably a half-dozen ministers and psychologists. They listened patiently to my complaints, told me I should mature, sympathized with me in all my trials and tribulations, and showed me the door. Each time I left as confused and cynical as when I arrived, and I always wondered why these counselors felt they had something to contribute to troubled people.

Then at Sunday school, after a series of lessons on "How to Have a Life That Matters," I heard of a religious experiment devised by the teacher while in earnest and desperate prayer. The teacher said he knew his Sunday school class had energy and talent that could be put to use for God, but he hadn't been able to channel it. He had prayed about this matter and in some moments of inspiration, he wrote out the program of the "Ten Brave Christians."

When I first heard about the experiment, I felt an immediate urge to "try it," but because all my friends were anything but spiritually minded, I knew they would tease me. I also felt I would never be able to pray in public or witness to others. I have always been mortally afraid to speak a word in front of a group.

To my surprise, my husband expected from the beginning that I would join the group. He said, "If this can change your life, you'll be able to witness." On the last day before the experiment started, I decided to try it.

You see, I had tried everything else. I had tried painting (I thought I was to be another Rembrandt, for awhile). I had tried partying (I just woke up with another hangover). I had even tried church work, (it seemed no one at that church did anything right, but me).

As a last resort, I decided to put everything I had into the Great Experiment.

The first two days (Monday and Tuesday) I felt very noble and good, getting up at 5:30 and doing those good deeds, etc. Then, Tuesday night at the group meeting I picked as my inspirational book *Prayer Can Change Your Life*. That night I sat up until the early hours of the morning reading that book. It is a very scientific account of how a psychologist took three groups of troubled people. One group prayed as they had always prayed and got no response in a given time. The second group was given the help of psychology and got a limited response. The third group combined psychology with prayer, according to the author's formula. This group found an amazing amount of help. Some were cured of illnesses, such as ulcers, asthma, etc.; others improved their relationships with those around them—wives, mothers-in-law, etc.

I found a manila pad and began to write down all of the people I disliked. I even included some I actually hated. It was quite a list. I was shattered by making that list. I taped the sheets together and held them up. The list was as tall as I was. Then, while crying so hard I could barely see to write, I wrote my name at the bottom of the list.

Wednesday morning during my 5:30 session, I tried to pray as outlined in the book. I prayed as I had never prayed before. I brought up honestly all the sins that I had tried to hide from myself for years; all the guilt, all the fears, all the worries. This was the most painful experience of my life, and that Wednesday was the most painful day of my life.

On Thursday morning, I finally went to the church, ostensibly to do my two hours' work, but really to talk to the pastor. I poured out to him my doubts about God, and he helped me to begin to understand how juvenile my ideas were about God. I cried that day until I felt that if I did not find God, I would lose my mind. That afternoon, while doing the family ironing—and crying a lot—I had what I felt was a completely new and original idea: *God is love*! That was so "new" an idea to me that I was overwhelmed! God was not in the clouds, or next door, or with the preacher: God was in my heart and God's love was flowing over me like waves in the ocean! How could I ever explain my joy on that day?

I had found a reason for living! I had found a peace I had never thought was possible. The wonder and joy I felt were so immense that words could not express it! I felt God's love pouring through my body and pulsing through my veins. I loved everybody and I wanted to tell them of my discovery. I felt like writing to the president of the United States, telling him I had discovered the answer to all problems.

As I went about my tasks on Friday, the answers to all the questions I had been worrying about for years came pouring into my consciousness so rapidly I simply could not digest them all at once. I would think, "I'll put that idea aside until I have time to think about it." I wanted to stop people on the street and tell them, "God is love!" I had found God, but I knew they wouldn't understand what I was talking about.

When I came across a troubled person on that day, his troubles seemed to hit me like a physical blow. I could see God shining out of my children's eyes (and the eyes of other children, too), and I could feel my love for the children simply radiating out of them. I felt that if I could only turn my eyes inward, I would be able to see God face-to-face. I had such a strong feeling of God's presence that I actually looked in the mirror and was surprised to see that I had not changed at all.

I never expect to have an experience like that again until I die. In fact, that day I thought, "This is what Heaven will be like, only more so." And I still believe this to be true.

On Saturday afternoon, as daily cares and trials began piling in again, I began to lose that strong sense of God's presence and became temporarily depressed. I felt that God was leaving me, and although I prayed very hard, I wasn't able to regain the joyous feeling. It took about two weeks for the feeling to completely wear off, but I was left with a sense of complete dedication and trust in God. I am not able to keep my faith pure, and sometimes I am very discouraged with myself for straying from what I know I should do. I feel so humble when I realize that anything I do for God is less than an atom when compared with what God has done for me. Lowly me, who doesn't really deserve anything at all— all I have ever done is exist, with nothing good to show for my thirty-two years but two beautiful, fine boys, who after all are only gifts from God.

I am learning everyday more about God's plan for me. Everyday is an adventure, as exciting as it was when I was a child.

When I look back over the last few months and realize how my life has been changed, I can hardly believe it. But I know the only way I can continue is to put faith in God first, love for others second, and my own ego and pride down, down, down. If I can be as an empty vessel and invite Christ in, there is no end to how He can use me. In this way God has already touched the lives of some of my friends and close relatives.

When I give myself to God's direction for the day, it is unbelievable how smoothly the day runs. Even the little things, such as finding parking places, finding people in when I call, and many other little incidents seem to click into place. When I am about to do something that is not God's will, I feel an uncomfortable twinge and there is no doubt in my mind that I should not do it. The one time I went ahead and did what I knew I shouldn't do, someone ended up in the hospital as a result!

Here I Go Again
Elizabeth DuBois Russo

Elizabeth shared her story with me on e-mail.

In March of 1985, I was finishing the last semester of law school at Washington University in St. Louis, about to turn thirty, experiencing crises in my personal life, and physically rundown. I was at a major crossroad. I was receiving counseling from a very good therapist, and trying to stay with an aerobics program. And I went to church on Sundays. But something was terribly wrong. I always felt that God was in my life, but something was missing.

I had been hearing about the John Wesley Great Experiment that our church was going to be conducting during the month of March. It sounded intriguing: "Wanted: Ten Brave Christians." Although I'm sometimes lazy about mundane things, if you put Mt. Everest in front of me I say, "Let's go"! This sounded like a challenge. But what finally hooked me was a young mother about my age witnessing from the pulpit one morning. She spoke intelligently and passionately about being a strong-willed woman who was working hard for success and wanting a strong family life and a life that matters. She spoke of learning how to put God first in her life and how it wasn't easy, but she spoke of many gifts given to her in return. After the worship service, I attended a brief but serious meeting outlining the expectations of undertaking this program. I felt like I was joining the Marines or signing on to be a monk in the fourteenth century, but it struck me as something I had to do.

Over the weeks that followed, I struggled with the issue of prayer. I felt that I had always talked to God, but that it was my own little secret. The prayers that I had grown up knowing I tended to mumble thoughtlessly, with my mind turned elsewhere. And those prayers would only be heard on Sundays or at the dinner table (occasionally) or sometimes at night when I felt my daughter should be brought up right. But I wasn't listening and I wasn't really opening myself up for communication. And while I at first thought of many reasons why I shouldn't have to get up at 5:30 in the morning and pray on my knees and really think about it, I had committed to do these very things and I was determined. The changes in my life during and after those weeks were subtle, yet profound.

I was still struggling, but I had the most powerful tool one could have—the power of prayer. Through prayer and the communion with people I met in my group (there were twelve of us) I learned to really examine my life and give it meaningful direction. I reacquainted myself with the notion of thinking and caring for others and added a new twist (for me)—doing things for them without expectation of thanks or recognition.

Best of all, I have learned to really open myself up to talking to God, and when words fail me, to say, "Show me the way, Lord" and then *listen*. The answer always comes. Sometimes, I had to be told or shown many times before I got it, but I feel the gift of peace that comes with knowing that sooner or later the answer will come.

Thirteen years later, I am excited about re-upping again. I have spoken many times of how this Great Experiment has changed my life, and am excited that this year my church in Connecticut is willing to undertake it.

Discipline Two at Work
WORK AT LEAST TWO HOURS IN THE CHURCH
EACH WEEK

Spiritual Growth at Maggie Jones
Memorial United Methodist Church
John Hitz

John Hitz is employed by the Tennessee Department of Health.

How the Holy Spirit began to move among us!

In March of 1995, I promised to help the chairperson of our spiritual formation committee introduce The John Wesley Great Experiment program, which I had participated in every March since 1990. I briefly explained the experiment and the seed was planted. Nine people responded. The Great Experiment was the kindled ember that was needed within this body of Christ. Our weekly prayer time in the group became a bonded nucleus within the church and the emphasis which was needed to ignite the remainder of the church family. As the month came to a close, two very significant events took place.

The first was a workday for the "two hours of work each week." While a contractor was painting the outside of the church, the congregation painted the inside—those who were participating in the group and some who were not. The church had not been painted in fourteen years. Later in the month, the curtains were washed and ironed. Others cleaned windows, cleaned and organized shelves, several of the men installed two iron railings at a side entrance, pews were polished, floors were swept and mopped, the carpet was vacuumed, and food and drinks were prepared for our lunch and snack times. Without at first realizing what was happening, we were receiving the empowerment of the Holy Spirit, and everyone felt that each was being conformed into the image of Christ for others.

The other event that occurred during the John Wesley Great Experiment took place the last Monday in March. I had also been participating with a Great Experiment group at my home church. Both churches had exchanged names with each other for prayer, but they only knew each other as a name on a piece of paper. I proposed to each group that on the last Monday in the month we all meet as a combined group at Maggie Jones Church. It would be a time for prayer, for sharing experiences that had occurred during the month, and for fellowship between the two churches. The Holy Spirit blessed each person who attended that evening.

As the year progressed, there were several events, which denoted new life and enthusiasm as the Holy Spirit continued to move us and move in us:

1. A new roof was put on the church after fifteen years.
2. Special music during the worship service began to be more frequent.
3. A Bible study group was begun on Sunday evenings by the lay leader of the church.
4. Attendance at Sunday worship began to increase, and eventually, nearly doubled.
5. Another Bible study group was begun on Wednesday mornings for the women of the church.
6. The idea of discernment and consensus was reintroduced for our church conference.
7. At Christmas, the congregation assembled a float for the youth to ride in the Christmas parade.
8. All churches in the community were invited to a New Year's Eve service, a potluck dinner, and Eucharist. Three youth were baptized that evening.
9. I completed requirements to become a part-time pastor and was appointed to Maggie Jones Memorial Church.

How the Holy Spirit moves!

Discipline Three at Work
GIVE GOD A TENTH OF ONE'S EARNINGS FOR THE MONTH

My Story
John E. (Jack) Turner

Jack Turner and Iris were charter members of John Wesley United Methodist Church.

When the Ten Brave Christian challenge was first presented to us at John Wesley Church in the spring of 1965, it appealed to me, except the part about tithing. Because of unusual financial demands at that time, I decided to pass on it. But when Danny made the call on the following Sunday, I went to the altar and made a commitment that I have never regretted.

The Ten Brave Christian discipline made me look at myself as I had never done before, and I did not like what I saw.

It literally turned my life around. I, of course, tithed for that month and have done so, and more, ever since. My wife, Iris, did not commit to participate in the program, so she did not tithe her income that month. But she soon began to tithe and we have both done so since. Tithing is just a part of our lives. We give off of the top and never stop to ask, "Can we afford it?" It has never been hard for us, though in retirement (both of us retired in 1977) our income has been meager compared to today's incomes. Money has never been a problem. As one of our former pastors, Tom Farmer, would say, "Thank you, Jesus."

I have gone through the Ten Brave Christian program twice since 1965, and I have been renewed and blessed each time, but nothing like that original month in 1965. It was truly a spiritual awakening like nothing I have ever experienced. I will always be grateful. It has helped me to be a better Christian in all that I have done since. Thanks be to God!

Discipline Four at Work
**SPEND FROM 5:30 TO 6:00 EACH MORNING
IN PRAYER AND MEDITATION**

Meeting with God, Daily
James and Katherine Goode

James and Katherine Goode are longtime, faithful Christians in Florida.

Following a Lay Witness Mission at Palm Springs (U)MC, Hialeah, Florida, in September 1971, my wife (Katherine "Kat") and I wanted to become disciples of Jesus Christ. We were joined by eight others in a prayer group. We were using the little book *A Life That Really Matters* by Danny E. Morris.

After a few days into this Ten Brave Christian program, our pastor, Bill Swygert, invited Danny (who was serving as pastor of a nearby church) to bring a few laypersons from his church who had gone through this course to meet with our group. Danny shared some insights and thoughts with us for a few minutes before introducing our other guests and offering us the opportunity to ask questions.

I knew that Kat was struggling with getting up for Bible study at 5:30 A.M. She didn't understand why she could not just get up "an hour earlier than usual." We had three young children who placed a lot of demands on her time and energy. Since she was a little shy, I asked about this for her. Danny called on an elderly woman to share her experience about the early morning prayer time.

She said that at first she had struggled with the same problem, but God revealed to her that she had an appointment with *Him* (along with nine other people in her group) at 5:30 A.M. That answer helped Kat to realize the importance of meeting with God daily at a specific time. After that realization, Kat never had a problem with getting up at 5:30 A.M. to meet with

God. Almost twenty-six years later, she continues to meet with God for an hour or more in the very early morning.

Discipline Five at Work
WITNESS FOR GOD THEIR EXPERIENCES TO OTHERS

The Mayor
Sam Teague as told to Danny Morris

Sam related this experience to us during the first week of our original Great Experiment group.

As mayor of Tallahassee, Sam and other city officials had struggled over a pesky problem that no one had solved: how to keep a dependable night janitor for the new airport. There were many complaints about the dirty terminal. Several attempts had failed, and the little problem remained unsolved for so long, it had become a "big" problem. However, the man who was currently employed had been doing a good job for several months.

Sam was making a 6:15 flight to Atlanta and decided to go to the airport early enough to have a visit with this worker. Because of the relative smallness of the airport, the mayor went walking about and found the man mopping the floor in one end of the terminal. He walked up and told him his name, shook hands with him, and said, "I am the mayor and I want to thank you for the good job you are doing. I thank you on behalf of all of our citizens."

The janitor just stood there without saying a word.

Again Sam shook his hand and called him by name, saying, "Thank you, Mr._____."

Tears were welling up in the fellow's eyes. He was finally able to get his words out.

"Thank you. I can't remember when anyone has told me I am doing a good job."

That was a powerful and unforgettable moment for the janitor and for Sam. And it was the same for our group. We had just heard the story of a Christian witness, which came right up out of Sam's life situation, out of who he was and what needed to be done.

So this is what a Christian witness is! There was nothing scary about that. It was natural. A little effort was required, but the result was worth the effort. We began to feel that any of us could do "something like that." No tracts were passed out, no Bible was thumped or shaken in anyone's face. No accusing finger of judgment was pointed. No one had been embarrassed. All in all, it had been a good experience for both of them. One person had communicated to another person a sense of caring, concern, and appreciation. None of us doubted that Christ was present in that early morning meeting.

Here are two additional witnesses that were written by Mike and Becky Waldrop, who were members of our church, St. Paul UMC in Mt. Juliet, Tennessee, when they participated in the John Wesley Great Experiment. Their stories have not been placed within any one of the five disciplines. They have been placed together because, beyond the power of their individual witnesses to their faith, they tell two parts of the same story.

A Funny Thing Happened on Our Way to Hong Kong
J. Michael Waldrop

Becky and I had just returned from living overseas as expatriots. I was a management consultant for a United States firm consulting in Asia. Exciting as it was, life overseas had been a very difficult and dry time for both of us spiritually. Then came the Great Experiment, "Wanted: Ten Brave Christians." We knew we had to be involved, drawn in by a shared feeling of urgency. We were expecting to go back to Hong Kong after a couple of years of living stateside while our son, Jonathan, finished high school. We wanted to be better prepared spiritually for life far from home, family, and the spiritual support of a congregation. This, we believed, explained the strong sense of urgency that we must do this experiment. The opportunity for participating in a small group and for a renewed prayer life were exactly the things we had been looking for.

At first it appeared to be impossible for me to participate in this group because of my work and travel schedule. Even though I could not attend the first meeting because of my work commitments, Becky attended. Once the group met, they agreed to meet on Friday nights. Usually, this was the night I was sure to be home. But in the end, we never met at that time. We met instead on Sunday nights. For thirty days we got up at 5:30 A.M., every day. We prayed and meditated for thirty minutes—reading scripture, and praying for specific concerns for each other. And we planned one anonymous good deed to do for someone else each day. We committed to give two hours each week in service to the church, and we committed to tithe our income for one month. We also met once a week to share how things were going. We committed to witness about our experience.

The results are impossible to describe in a few words. Something unbelievable began to happen to the members of our group as we prayed. Not only were our prayers answered, not only did God use each of us to effect loving changes in others, but Becky and I began to change. Feelings of love and power began to surround us all. We were opening up, taking risks, reaching out in new, courageous ways. We were also beginning to realize that something was happening that was very important and greater than we had expected. We were beginning, slowly and fearfully at first, to surrender ourselves to the God who made us and knows us and loves us beyond our understanding. It would be a life's work to appropriate the full meaning of this discovery, but we had made a beginning together. We had several Great Experiment groups going on at once in our church. The wind of the Spirit began to blow through the entire church—binding, healing, and challenging.

No one was affected more than I was. In just those short thirty days, God made it possible for me to renew and heal my relationship with my father. It was a difficult and painful process because I did not really *know* my dad. But in the act of reaching out, trying to know him, both of my parents responded with love and forgiveness. And it seemed to be a key that unlocked my own capacity for love. It was a new freedom; it was life renewing. Oh, I had always cared for people. I am gentle by nature, but I had always protected myself—that inner core. Now I was capable of a more compassionate, loving relationship, opening myself to others . . . to intimacy . . . to God. When the thirty days were over, there were so many miracles in our group, all of us became convinced of the power of prayer. When the group discussed continuing, we were led to meet monthly for the next two years. The John Wesley Great Experiment was the beginning of our intense journey toward a more committed life of discipleship.

It was the group that served as a "Clearness Committee" when Becky and I sought clarity in my answering God's call to ordained ministry. It seems that we did not need to prepare for a return trip to Asia after all. We had found a whole new life instead—a life of ministry in Christ. In the years that followed, through seminary, through all the extraordinary people that God brought into our lives, through prayer and struggle, and through the work of love, we continued to experience God's grace—a grace which overwhelmed us and sustained us and claimed us as God's own. Becky has discovered her own special call to discipleship as an artist working in spiritual formation and worship. As a couple and as individuals we have discovered more grace, more freedom, and more meaning for our lives than we ever knew was possible.

Becky and I introduced The John Wesley Great Experiment at my first appointment as an associate pastor. We recognized an intense hunger for spiritual growth in the congregation, very much like what we had felt. What we had experienced through the Holy Spirit began to work in the church to change lives as they, too, discovered the power of prayer and practiced the five disciplines for their thirty days. To date, more than seventy members have begun this journey of spiritual growth in our church. Some of the covenant groups are still meeting. Many have become the newly empowered leaders in our congregation—answering God's call on their lives and discovering new identities in Christ Jesus.

We have come to believe that there is a great hunger in the church and in the world for a deeper experience of God. We know of no better starting place for those just beginning their journey of faith, and no better place for renewal for those further along on the journey, than The John Wesley Great Experiment. We should offer this as a cheerful warning: *Be careful. These thirty days could change your life*.

Patchwork Table
Becky Waldrop

It was a bad time in our church—a time of conflict and dissatisfaction—a time of changes long overdue. We all showed up at the administrative board meetings fully prepared—each of us with our own *Book of Discipline* held firmly in our laps, sure of our positions, holding those who were a bit less sure in contempt, and arguing with Pharisaical glee. We made sure our alliances were secure and our points well made. The board meetings were the best attended in years.

While we were feeling the heavy responsibilities of running the church and beginning to be a little alarmed at how mean other people could become at our board meetings, someone was beginning something called the John Wesley Great Experiment. The newsletter article said, "Wanted: Ten Brave Christians!" It was right next to the yearly announcement that the United Methodist Women (UMW) were planning their fall bazaar.

This year the UMW's project was more important than usual. There had been a noticeable decline in the giving of our congregation and an ensuing financial crunch. Someone had the idea that it would be nice if all the women would make a single quilt to auction off at the bazaar. It would be a "big ticket" item and seemed easy enough to do if everyone helped. A few of the real quilters made little "kits" in plastic bags for others to assemble into individual squares. These would be returned and put together to construct the quilt.

I was not active in the UMW, but I did take four of their little unassembled squares to do because I could not refuse the women who asked. I loved them, you see. Not being a quilter, I was somewhat concerned as to how I would put the pieces together, but they had thought of that and provided an instruction sheet in each packet. I took the little bags of gold and brown calico pieces home with me. I also did something even more risky than that— I decided I would begin the John Wesley Great Experiment when it started the following month. It was very unlike me.

I worked and worked on those four quilt squares in the interim. The instructions were great, but no matter how I tried, I could *not* get the squares to work out the same size as the pattern called for. I even took one apart and reassembled it, but it was no use. I felt really badly about it and wondered whether they could even use my eccentric little squares that wouldn't measure out right and looked a little worn and frayed from my feverish efforts. But I took them back to church (not knowing what else to do with them) and gave them to my friends with profuse apologies. They just smiled at me and showed me a lot of other squares they had received. Some were even a worse mess than mine—more like triangles than squares! Some had the different colors in all the wrong places. Some seemed to be coming apart at the seams already. I went away feeling very sorry for whoever might attempt to put all those defective squares together. I was certain that there would be no quilt at the bazaar. As for the John Wesley Great Experiment, I felt somewhat less "brave" than I had before. Maybe I really was too busy with the problems of the church right now to be out yet another night of the week praying.

I missed the bazaar itself, but was surprised to hear that one of the women of the church bought the quilt. It wasn't until Thanksgiving weekend that I had the chance to see it. It was on the altar that Sunday. Someone had spread it there in a special Thanksgiving arrangement. Spilling out across it were all the fruits of the harvest, a cornucopia of plenty, a riotous celebration of God's faithfulness and grace. And, in the center, sitting atop our many calico squares, was the chalice and a loaf of fresh bread.

Quite suddenly the image of that patchwork table pierced my "Let's all make nice, its Sunday" consciousness and seemed to explode inside me. I wanted to stand up and shout: "Look! A miracle! Can't you see it?" For our squares were altogether. It was a quilt and it was beautiful!

As the communion liturgy began and I watched our congregation file down, one-by-one to dip their bread into the same cup, I mentally deposited my *Book of Discipline* back in its spot on the shelf. For here, finally, was the church. Here was the body of Christ—all of us, without exception, as eccentric and broken as those funny, shabby little squares in our quilt. And here was the quilt—mysteriously and wondrously sewn together with loving hands.

I sat through the whole service with tears on my cheeks. It no longer mattered now which squares were mine—for I was a part of something new and suddenly achingly real to me—a community of faith. God's people—the body of Christ, our Lord. Perhaps others saw it, too—I don't know. No one stood up and shouted that day. . . . But soon after that we began to lose interest in our tiny power struggles. First, three of us gathered on a Monday morning—then we Ten Brave Christians gathered to pray—on a Sunday evening, then twenty of us—then many, many more. The Great Experiment had finally begun and for thirty days we were doing it for real. We were learning to pray . . . some of us for the first time in our lives. We prayed for each other. We prayed for ourselves. We prayed for our church, and a wind began to blow through its buildings. Changes were made and a community of

God's people stood up, and began, at first timidly, and then grad-
ually more boldly to bring all those pieces of themselves and place
them in very loving and very powerful hands. Amen.

A Retrospective
Dr. Thomas E. Farmer Jr.

*Tom Farmer Jr., who is currently senior minister at St. Paul United
Methodist Church in Largo, Florida, brought back the challenge of the
Great Experiment to John Wesley United Methodist Church.*

In June of 1972, when I was appointed pastor of John Wesley
(U)MC in Tallahassee, Florida, the most amazing thing I
discovered upon arrival was the absence of "The Ten Brave
Christian Program." I had heard of the dynamic impact of this
month-long discipline of practicing the basics of our faith and
had looked forward to being the pastor of the church where
God birthed this opportunity for spiritual renewal through Sam
Teague and Danny Morris, the pastor of John Wesley. Much to
my dismay and surprise, I found that the experiment in discipleship had been dormant in the church for several years.
When some friends and colleagues found out about my appointment to John Wesley, they joked and jived, "Oh yeah—that's
where you can find ten brave Christians, if you're lucky!" Or, on
a kinder note, some would ask, "Isn't that the church where the
Ten Brave Christian movement started?" Still others said, "Let
me know what happened to the ten brave followers of Jesus!"
Upon arrival I did just that—I found them! As a matter of
fact, what I found was that although the experiment was no
longer being emphasized, the men and women who were in
the initial groups with Sam and Danny were still among the
"remnant" of faithful, sincere, and accountable members of the
Lord's Church! So my answer was quickly formed for those who
had suspected that this experiment attracted religious fanatics
and divided the church: "Yes, the Ten Brave Christians are still

here—tithing, praying, loving God, and serving His church!"

On the first Sunday in July 1972, I invited those who would like to, to join me in a month of the Ten Brave Christians Program—and much to my heart's delight, the altar filled with faithful folk who were hungry for more of God, Jesus, and the Holy Spirit! Twenty-two persons came forward at the close of the service. That was exactly the number that was in the first group in 1965.

Since that first Sunday in July of 1972, and to this hour, I have utilized the Great Experiment in every church I have served as pastor, and with the same results: cleansing, renewal, revival, restoration, and deepening of the lives of the persons who dared to put God first for one month!

There will always be suspicious scoffers along the sidelines when any serious attempt at spiritual renewal is made. The sad thing is that these persons usually stay right there—on the sidelines, never taking up for themselves the challenge made by our Lord to "Follow me." And it is even sadder that they never find the joy that awaits an accountable surrender to the Lord and deepening of the walk of faith.

Across these twenty-six years I have offered the Ten Brave Christian Experiment to the three congregations that I have served, and literally hundreds of lives have been greatly blessed and dozens have been eternally changed by participating in this experiment. I have yet to find one person who stayed with the program for the entire month that has anything but praise and thanksgiving to God for having participated.

Chapter Six

Better than a
Jump Start

◆

SCENARIO NO. 1

"Hey, I am excited over something I want to tell you about that will be good to do in our prayer group. I think you will agree that this is the kind of challenge we have been looking for. It's called the Great Experiment, and the thing I like about it is that it only lasts a month.

Here are the five challenges:

Wanted: Ten Brave Christians,
who for one month
1. Will meet once each week to learn how to pray.
2. Will give two hours' time each week to God.
3. Will give God 1/10 of their earnings.
4. Will spend from 5:30 to 6:00 each morning in prayer and meditation.
5. Will witness for God their experience to others.

Let's do this as a group. We can start tomorrow morning!"
Jump start? Forget it!

SCENARIO NO. 2

It will be better if one gets excited and gives their excitement a chance to grow. The Great Experiment is a significant spiritual formation challenge for a congregation and it should be handled accordingly. It is a bold challenge to *put God first* in our lives through authentic and powerful spiritual disciplines. Many people have said that the *five* are like spiritual dynamite. We would not handle actual dynamite carelessly, and we must not handle *spiritual* dynamite carelessly.

Your church will benefit by successively focusing on one of the disciplines each Sunday. Then, on the sixth Sunday, invite persons to respond to be in a Great Experiment group. Interpret each discipline carefully so all can determine if they wish to participate in a group that will experiment with the disciplines. In fact, this is a good word to use in referring to the challenge—the Great Experiment.

A jump start will not do!

Consider each of the spiritual disciplines on its own merit. As you present successive points of the challenge each Sunday, people will begin to view them cumulatively. Each is strong in itself, but when they are practiced together, they build strength like matches do when several are tied together with a string.

Order enough copies of *A Life That Really Matters* (see page 98) to accommodate the size of your congregation: twenty books for a small-membership church; forty books for a medium-size church; sixty to one hundred books for a large-membership church. (Also, order enough copies of *The John Wesley Great Experiment* booklet so each participant can have one.) During the interpretation and challenge period ask people to check out a book to read about how the Great Experiment started, the details of the challenge, and what some participants have said about it. Ask everyone who checks out a book to read it within two or three days and return it so others can check it out. Encourage as many as possible to read the book during the six weeks' challenge and interpretation period.

Order two (or three or five, according to size of your congregation) audiotapes that interpret the challenge. The cassette tape, entitled, "The Miracle Caught on Tape" provides excellent content on the five disciplines.

Forget a jump start!

TO SUNDAY SCHOOL TEACHERS

You may wish to check out a cassette tape and play several brief portions for your class. Call for a discussion on one or several Sundays of the challenge period by using any of the following questions:

1. In terms of what we just heard (on the cassette), what would be the hardest part of the challenge for you?
2. What would be easiest?
3. How do you feel about *discipline*, generally?
4. How do you feel about *spiritual* discipline?
5. Have any of you ever focused on a spiritual discipline by practicing it for a time? Will you tell us about your experience with it?
6. What seems unreasonable about the spiritual discipline we just heard about?
7. What seems reasonable about it?
8. What type of persons do you think will be attracted by this challenge and will want to participate in a group?
9. What type would not be attracted to it?
10. Is the period of thirty days too short to do any good, or is the short time frame a positive point for you?

11. Have any of you heard about anyone who is thinking about, or has decided to participate?
12. We have some of the books here. Let's see how many want to read about the challenge. "George" or "Martha," will you make a list of who takes a book and who wants one, and help us keep them circulating?
13. Do you think we will find ten?
14. Will you be one?

Don't settle for a jump start!

TO THE CHURCH BOARD (OR OTHER APPROPRIATE GROUPS)

During this challenge period do all you can to invite and encourage as many as possible to read the book and/or to listen to the cassette tape. Each of you on the board may have more responsibility than anyone else to invite persons to consider the challenge to *put God first*. As a board member, call forth the best response in all areas of your influence.

But remember, this is a personal challenge, which means that your influence will be needed in two ways:

1. Encourage response, but do not push. Do not intimidate. Do not assume. Do not judge others. Some persons will surprise you with their response; others will disappoint you. Be positive and helpful, friendly, and loving, as you talk with others about the challenge. If (and when) you decide to participate, let your decision be known within the circle of your influence.
2. As a spiritual leader of the church, you have more than *official* responsibility for leadership. This invitation to *put God first* is a direct invitation to you, personally. We are hoping to find ten. Will you be one? It is a very personal challenge to you.

The church board needs more than a jump start!

TO PRESIDENTS OF THE WOMEN'S AND MEN'S ORGANIZATIONS AND ALL OTHER CHURCH ORGANIZATIONS

All of you are leaders. Your spiritual leadership in presenting this churchwide challenge will be profoundly helpful. Make the challenge a central part of your program and business meeting during the challenge period. For some persons, you will be the only leader that has their attention. Do all you can to encourage the people in your group to *put God first*.

A jump start may be quick, but it will not last!

TO YOUTH AND WORKERS WITH YOUTH

The Great Experiment is not just an "adult thing." Youth can (and hopefully will) have as much interest and need as anyone to *put God first* in their lives. Make the challenge a meaningful part of the youth experience in your church. The audiotape can be helpful. (See suggested questions listed for Sunday school teachers, page 78.)

Circulate the books and keep them moving from one to another so many youth will know the full meaning of the challenge.

There are actually two options for youth participation:

Option One

(For youth who are older—eleventh and twelfth grades and above)

Provide the youth with qualified adult leadership for a regular Great Experiment group like the book describes—almost the same format that an adult group will use. The only difference is that the youth base their tithe for the month on their income, whether they work or have an allowance. If they do not have a regular income, let them designate how much they will give and how they will earn it. (This becomes a covenant that they make with their group and the group encourages and celebrates their faithfulness to this part of their commitment.)

The youth Great Experiment group should always have competent and committed adult leadership who have the confidence of the youth.

Option Two

(For youth who are in middle school through the tenth grade)

They should be invited to participate in the "6:33 Club." (It is described in *A Life That Really Matters*, page 78.) If there is a mixed group of middle school, juniors, and seniors, the "6:33 Club" should be offered. (Juniors and seniors may also choose to enter into option two.) Youth deserve more than a jump start!

TO THE PASTOR OR PASTORS

Do not try to jump-start a group. The result is seldom worth the effort.

1. When persons enter into the potential of this challenge without understanding the implications of *putting God first* . . .
2. When they are enthusiastic but not informed . . .
3. When they become caught up in the moment by hearing someone else's enthusiasm or persuasion . . .
4. When they decide to do it because someone they like or admire is doing it . . .
5. When they respond on the spur of the moment . . .

. . . there is little reason to hope that it will be a meaningful experience—much less life-changing for them. That is what we are looking for here. *Putting God first* in one's life can be a life-changing experience!

Also, do not try to handpick a group of friends, church leaders, or persons you know who need this challenge. The result will likely backfire and the effort can become divisive.

Go churchwide with the challenge. Present it boldly. Teach it. Preach it. Aim for the greatest response that is possible. A five-Sunday series on the disciplines of the Great Experiment is a good way to present the challenge. Although the challenge can be presented more briefly, there is much preaching and teaching content within the five disciplines.

On the First Sunday

Preach about the first discipline, "Learning how to pray."

Talk about prayer in your own life, about great persons of prayer you have known, about how this prayer group will work, what it will be like to be in a group, and what such groups can mean to the church, and many other "calls to prayer." Assure everyone that they will learn about prayer and how to pray, but they will not be manipulated, embarrassed, or forced to pray, or have to pray aloud.

On the Second Sunday

Preach about "Service to God and to people."

Working at least two hours in the church each week is usually not a major threat. Two hours is not a long time, but it will be impressive if you multiply it out and show what an impact will be made by ten people who work two hours a week for four weeks. What if you had five, or ten, or twelve such groups—and additional groups in subsequent months.

Present your adapted list of things the church needs people to do, which appears on pages 23–24. Suggest that each person will be asked to select how they will work in the church two hours each week and keep up within their commitment each week.

Preach on *diakonia* (service) and *koinonia* (fellowship.) They are like two sides of the same coin.

On the Third Sunday

Preach and teach on tithing.

Tithing has been a major emphasis in the entirety of Judeo-Christian history and tradition. It is not well understood, and is actually misunderstood, by many of our people.

The John Wesley Great Experiment is an experiment in Christian tithing. Talk about practical aspects of tithing: how to figure the tithe—on gross or net income? Is one tithing while contributing to the upkeep of an elderly parent? What guidance can you give when the person in the group wants to tithe for the month and their mate does not want to? How can a nonemployed spouse participate when he or she earns no direct income, but feels a call or a desire to tithe?

Any of these considerations are wonderful prompts to the pastor in giving guidance that is theologically sound, practical, and helpful.

There are two additional dimensions of tithing which need to be clearly annunciated:

1. Take the tithe out first.
2. Pray about how you spend the other nine-tenths.

These are amazing rubics which have wonderful theological and practical gifts for the persons who actually practice them.

Keep the clear focus about tithing as it is practiced in the experiment. The commitment is to tithe for one month—*as an experiment*. Participants are frequently amazed about what can be spiritually experienced and learned about tithing, even in thirty (or thirty-one) days.

Pastor(s), do not miss the opportunity to give your people spiritual and practical guidance on this important subject.

You may need to jump-start your car, but do not jump-start the Great Experiment!

After the Third Sunday announce the "Come and See" meeting and the Commitment Sunday. They will be detailed later.

On the Fourth Sunday

Preach and teach about prayer, Bible study, doing a good deed, and how you want to build and develop your life. Make this a Sunday that everyone will remember.

The early morning devotional period is divided into three ten-minute segments. Before getting to the detail of that half hour, set the scene in everyone's imaginations:

An early morning devotional period;
A half hour, beginning at 5:30;
Anticipate the time by doing whatever is necessary:
    To have a prepared place,
    To get fully awake,
    To be present to God with the Word before your day begins!

Give details of the pattern of using the first ten minutes for studying and writing about a Scripture passage; the second ten minutes to pray about and write a good deed you will do for someone that day (name the deed and name the person); the third ten minutes write at least one thought per day about how you would like to build and develop your life.

Many persons will not have experience with a devotional period, especially that early in the day. As you make practical suggestions they will see how simple the practice is and they will be encouraged to do it.

It is only for a half hour.
It is only for thirty (or thirty-one) days.

Encourage your people to do it. All of us really want to know:

How to study the Bible, devotionally.
How to care for others who are special to us.
How to put God first!

Jump-start any of these? Heaven's no!
Continue to announce the "Come and See" meeting and the Commitment Sunday. Details are given below.

On the Fifth Sunday
Speak on witnessing.

For many people, witnessing will be the most frightening part of the challenge. As you present this part of the challenge, be enthusiastic and cheerful (even humorous). This attitude will help to relieve anxiety about this subject.

Also, define Christian witnessing. A simple definition: We witness only about what we have seen, or what we have heard, or what we have experienced, and know to be true. Illustrate with examples of persons they know who have a Christian witness, by telling of your experience of witnessing, and by naming some places or situations where a Christian witness is needed. Help them see that witnessing is as natural as breathing—once we have something to witness about.

Remind them that the group will provide a little "laboratory" for experimenting with witnessing, and encouraging everyone to try it.

Jump start? Not with something this important!

Announce the "Come and See" meeting again.

The Sixth Sunday
Commitment Sunday.

Commitment Sunday is the day everyone has been anticipating. Make it an upbeat and lively service. Review all of the parts of the challenge, annotating the high points in review. Include the youth! Call for a response:

Options
1. Invite persons to come forward and stand together as a group at the altar or chancel. (Sometimes, someone will be encouraged to respond when they see a particular person come forward.)

or

2. Invite persons to fill out the registration slip in the bulletin and put it in the offering plate or in a basket placed for the purpose.

or

3. Invite persons to mail in their commitment to join the group prior to _____ (set a final date after the following Sunday). This will allow a week and two Sundays for people to respond.

Announce a "Come and See" meeting to be held after the first Sunday for a commitment (sixth Sunday) and another to be held after the following Sunday (seventh Sunday). Announce the deadline for making the commitment to be in the group. Example: The deadline is defined by the mailed envelope being "postmarked by midnight" on Tuesday night after the seventh Sunday. That becomes the deadline for responding to be in the group. No one will be in the group who responds after the deadline.

This group is *officially closed* at the designated time. Later respondents will be asked to wait for the beginning of the next group.

The "Come and See" Meeting

Announce a "Come and See" meeting to close the preaching/teaching series. This meeting should last no more than one hour. Because several weeks have been devoted to presenting the challenge, some interested persons may have been absent one or more Sundays. At the meeting, present the total challenge in a brief and clear way and invite the persons who wish to participate to make their commitment as they kneel at the chancel. Provide a three-by-five-inch card for them to sign and note their selected times for the weekly group meeting.

The "Come and See" meeting should be announced for the week following the first Commitment Sunday, and a second "Come and See" meeting announced for immediately following the deadline for joining the group. Example: If the final deadline is Tuesday at midnight, the final "Come and See" meeting could be held on Wednesday or Thursday evening.

This meeting is to be attended by everyone (youth and adults) who are considering—or have decided—to be in a group. Announce leaders, locations, and the time for the meetings. Some of those attending the meeting will have already decided; others will not be sure. It is often helpful for everyone to hear about the entire challenge in one sitting. For any who missed a Sunday or so, such a review is often an encouragement to make a decision to participate.

Give a final invitation to respond by asking them to fill out their card, take it to the altar, and pray a prayer of commitment before they leave. The simple card should list their name, address, phone number, and their choice of the group they plan to attend.

Try to accomplish the following:

1. Adequately publicize the name of group leaders, and where and when the groups will meet.
2. Give ample opportunity for persons to respond to: the "Come and See" meeting, Sunday school classes, the deadline to mail in commitment forms, or to notify the pastor.
3. Publicize the final time for mailing the commitments.
4. Close the group for the month as of the final time for commitment. (Everyone needs to begin together.)
5. Insure that all groups "go underground" (see page 18) and that the code of confidentiality is strictly observed.
6. Announce all Great Experiment group meetings in the bulletin and newsletter, but do not "beat the drum" for or about the groups.
7. Plan to start new groups regularly.

Do your best to present a strong challenge. Do not waste your time presenting a nonchallenge.

Be grateful for anyone who responds. Do not be judgmental about any who do not respond. Do not try to force a decision on anyone.

YOUTH AND THE GREAT EXPERIMENT

The challenge to put God first often has an enthusiastic hearing among youth. When the challenge is given in the church, let there be a strong invitation to youth classes and youth groups. Neither the youth nor the church are well served if they are overlooked or neglected, as if this is only an "adult thing." Youth who are in the middle school (or junior high) as well as high school may respond naturally. If there is a wide age span, consider having a younger and an older group. About an hour should be sufficient for the weekly meeting of either group.

Great Experiment Group for Youth

If there are enough youth who wish to participate in a regular Great Experiment group format like the adults, select an adult leader and provide a regular Great Experiment group experience for the interested youth. Great care should be devoted to selecting an adult leader. The Great Experiment can be undertaken on the same basis as the adult version with one modification. Some youth can tithe their allowance or their personal income from work, while others may need to earn money to give. The youth who are not working designate an amount they will give to God each week in lieu of a tithe. They designate the amount and the means by which they will earn that amount, and record this data as a part of their spiritual commitment. Their commitment may be changed or reaffirmed each week.

The 6:33 Club

An alternate plan is a "youth modification" of the Great Experiment called "The 6:33 Club." The theme Scripture for

the group is Matthew 6:33: "Seek ye first the kingdom of God and his righteousness, and all other things will be added unto you." The general questions for the group meetings are:
The Kingdom of God:
- What is it?
- How do you find it?
- How do you recognize it?
- What do you do when you find it?
- How do you share it with others?

These thematic questions supplement the group's responses to the regular movements of the Great Experiment:
- praying and learning how to pray;
- working two hours in the church each week;
- tithing their income or their allowance;
- the half-hour period of prayer and Bible study (including the daily good deed and how "I will build and develop my life"); and
- witnessing for God about their experiences.

In the "6:33 Club" there are four notable alterations of the adult version of the Great Experiment:
1. As noted above, youth are encouraged to state an amount they will give in lieu of a tithe (for those who do not have an income upon which to tithe).
2. The time for morning study and meditation is 6:33 A.M. when they follow the regular half-hour schedule of the Great Experiment. (The group may choose an earlier time for their morning prayer and meditation period if 6:33 in the morning is not compatible with their school schedule.)
3. The duration of the group is for twenty-one days instead of one month.
4. Scripture passages for the "6:33 Club" are especially selected and marked among the passages usually used by an adult group.

An emphasis may be placed on memorization of the books of the Bible, and of certain selected passages of Scripture. Adult leadership for the "6:33 Club" must also be chosen with utmost care. Just any interested adult will not necessarily qualify to lead the youth group. The adult must have some youth-oriented skills, both learned and felt, and should know the language of youth and have the confidence of youth from the beginning. Youth leadership of a group is not recommended.

The "6:33 Club" is an exciting discipline and is well suited for the temperament of youth. It can produce dramatic results rather quickly because most youth do not yet have as many spiritual hang-ups as adults.

Let the groups begin!

Chapter Seven

How to Begin

◆

Begin with the pastor who longs for the members of the congregation to respond to a unique spiritual challenge. This is not to imply that the church has seldom or never been spiritually challenged. But it is to say that presenting the challenge of the Great Experiment—"Wanted: Ten Brave Christians"—will accomplish several worthwhile goals:

1. It is a short-term challenge. Ideally the churchwide period of challenge is presented over a four-to- six-week period. The invitation is to participate in the group for one month, although many groups choose to continue longer than a month.

2. The disciplines are spiritual dynamite. The disciplines appear to be simple—and they are—but in their uniqueness and simplicity they have great spiritual power. They set forth biblical foundations for beginning the spiritual life. Changes that come to persons are often for a lifetime, and many people continue practicing parts of the disciplines for a lifetime.

3. The Great Experiment is comprehensive. The disciplines are not all that the church is about, but when they are practiced together, they provide great spiritual power. Consider the varied challenges they present: learning to pray, serving in the church, tithing, praying and meditating on Scripture, meeting with a small group, doing a daily good deed, and building and developing your life.

4. It is for youth and adults. See the youth adaptation of the "6:33 Club" on page 78, and note the "6:33 Club" pages in the daily procedure booklet.

5. It is exceedingly personal. You deal with your own "stuff" within your life situation. You decide how far you want to go and how deep. You choose what you want to talk about in your group. You decide on the commitments you wish to make. You determine how much good you want to derive, period. Within the group, everyone is praying for you by name, daily. This fact alone can open windows of wonder. Group members begin to expect and recognize miracles in each other's lives. In our hearts we intend to support the church with our prayers, our presence, our gifts, and our service. All these commitments are actualized through this challenge.

6. It is powerfully corporate. There is great strength in corporate discipline. Here, you are not "pushed" along, but supported forward by the heroic or faltering efforts of others who are also putting God first. You begin actually to "see" your own strengths and weaknesses more clearly, as you move along with others who are trying to stand tall, but sometimes stumble. You learn a lot about yourself.

7. It is a "lifetime" opportunity. When you make the choice to *put God first*, you will have a lifetime not to regret it, but—on the contrary—to make the most of it.

Begin with a layperson, who will say, Come on, pastor, let's get serious about our relationship to God in Christ and how we love and serve people. We want to open up the Bible and let it speak to our deepest needs so our lives can be spiritually formed in Christ. Let our church specialize in making Christian disciples and sending them forth into the world. Teach us how to pray. Call us to deeper and deeper spiritual commitment. We want a new church in our present building. Please challenge us with real challenges because we are never challenged by "nonchallenges."

Begin with the pastor, who will call for even one or two (or twelve or fifty) laypersons to stretch themselves to fit the challenge of living profoundly spiritual and fruitful lives.

Just to see the possibilities of that!

And to want that!

Such is a beginning!

We are saying that *somebody* needs to feel a hunger for a spiritually transformed life. *That is a beginning*. If no one feels that hunger, perhaps no one wants to change.

Unless you *want* to change, you never will!

Realistically, we must face the fact that not every person who tries the Great Experiment will have a dramatically transformed life. The reason—not every person will finally surrender his or her life to God though Christ in a given month. And without complete and total surrender, God cannot completely transform a life.

If you were to become a member of such a group and your group experienced about the same response as other groups, this is what you might look forward to:

- One-third of your group would have transformed lives.
- One-third would be deeply affected, and along with the first one-third, would want to continue.
- About one-third would not be too deeply affected. They would come to the end of the month with a somewhat bewildered feeling or a feeling that "nothing happened."

Of the first two-thirds of your group, all that needs to be said is that they will have found the secret to a happy life (*not to be happy, but to have a life that matters*) and if they continue to put God first in their lives and love God with all of their heart, all of their mind, and all of their strength, they will never go back to their old way of living.

Of the last one-third to whom "nothing happened," we now know that if they will try and try again (with special emphasis on learning how to pray) some of them will sooner or later surrender their lives to God and discover a new life. A common characteristic of this latter one-third is that they are "waiting" for something to happen—waiting for God to bring about a sudden miracle in their lives. Generally, it does not come this way. When it does come, it will be the result of some specific effort on their part to become aware of God and serve God by the surrender of their lives to God's will.

When any of you (or all of you) are ready, take on the whole church. Go churchwide with the challenge rather than to a select group—whether it be "the leaders," favorites of the pastor, the insiders, or even a "test" group. Go churchwide from the pulpit by preaching a series of sermons on each of the disciplines. *Teach* as you preach—about how to pray, how to tithe, how to serve, how to love and care, and how to grow spiritually!

Throughout the challenge period, make frequent *announcements* designating the day when the group(s) will start. Repeat over and over the specifics of getting the group(s) underway. Describe the various ways persons may make a response. Make it clear that you will be calling for a decision "to put God first" in specific ways for thirty days—*just to see what will happen*.

Keep in mind the word *cheerful*. Be cheerful as you present the challenge. These spiritual disciplines are not legalisms, demands, or even requests. They are invitations to grace *through* grace. Do not present the challenge harshly or with the slightest hint of anxiety or pressure. *You extend the invitation, God does the calling.* It is often the "stranger" or the most unlikely person who hears the call and responds. You are not asking people to do something strange. This experiment is not for a lifetime. People could "hold their breath for a month" if they had to.

And the *five* are practical. No one will have to quit their jobs or leave their homes or sell their boats. Everyone can practice the *five* and keep right on with their lives—but probably with some changes.

Even a small-membership church may need twenty copies of the book, *A Life That Really Matters*. Order enough books (see page 98 for details) so that you can adequately resource your church within the month while the challenge period is underway. The goal is that "just about everyone who wants to" will have read the book before the month begins. Reading all about the challenge is important because there is far more to it than one will discover just by reading the five disciplines. A good understanding makes long friendships, and understanding all that is involved here makes good Great Experiment groups. Either let the church buy the books and circulate them, or circulate the books by selling them. The more persons who read and understand the challenge, the better will be the response.

Toward the last of the period of preparation, the Commitment Form (see page 90) should be copied and made available upon request to all who are interested. (There is value in having the interested person request the Commitment Form, but you have the option of making it generally available.) There are always some persons whose decision is fleeting. The best procedure is to ask the interested person to take the form home, fill it out, and mail it to the person in your group who is selected to receive the written commitments. Not everyone will follow through. Always there are persons who say something like this: "You know, I meant to be a part of this prayer group, but I just never got around to filling out the form." But those who do "get around" to making their commitment in this way are really interested, and their desire and/or sense of need makes a difference.

The "Morning Prayer and Meditation Schedule" (see page 91) should be copied and made available to each participant. Whereas the Scripture readings for the first month (see page 92) deal with personal faith in the short scope of a few verses, the second-month Scriptures passages (see page 93), for those who desire to continue, are somewhat different in purpose. These longer passages point to mental and spiritual qualities of the Christian life. It is suggested that the related passages before and after each specific reference in the selections for the second month be read and incorporated in one's morning meditation and prayer.

A notebook for keeping this spiritual diary will become a treasure to each participant. The booklet, *The John Wesley Great Experiment*, is available for this purpose.

Finally, this fact must be faced: *There is absolutely no substitute for concerned and consecrated laypersons who want for themselves and their church a life that really matters. Let them come forward and join with their pastor in presenting the challenge to a deeper commitment in Christ.*

Let the pastor join with them in sounding the uncompromised gospel call to Christian commitment. This emphasis cannot be delegated as a responsibility. There must be at least one person—lay or clergy—who will put God first in his or her own life and lovingly, patiently, and prayerfully invite others to do the same.

After the preaching and teaching period there comes the experiment. But do not try to jump-start a group in order to get something going quickly. If you were to describe briefly the challenge and announce on Sunday that a group would begin the following Wednesday, you would probably have a greater response than if you present it for a month or more. But the "fallout" would be far greater within the jump-start group. This invitation is not just to form a unique new group, or to do something spiritual, but to "put God first," and that is a serious matter.

Observation: Being a member of a dead church, a dying church, a sleeping church, a weak church, a sick church, or a pitiful church is not nearly as good, or as much fun, or as exciting, as being in a church that is alive and loving, serving, growing, seething with spiritual ferment, hope, and promise. I know, because I have been in all of the above.

The one thing that is required to do away with the bad of a church is to enhance the *good* of a church by *putting God first* in the church.

Anyone who will!

As many as will!

Whenever they will!

For as long as they will!

Appendices

Questions Often Asked

1. What is the purpose of the Great Experiment group? It provides a covenant community that can help guide persons in their desire and commitment to put God first. It is a safe place to experiment with authentic spiritual principles. It is also like a spiritual rocket booster and often launches persons into ministry.

2. How long should I remain in the group? For at least a month, for as long as it is meaningful to you and you are growing spiritually, and until you are well on your way to doing what God calls you to do.

3. How long should the group continue? For as long as it has life . . . and spirit . . . and passion . . . and power. One group has continued for twenty-two years. This is a very unusual group and is not the norm or the goal. Because of its longevity, the people in this group kept changing because some dropped out and others joined. But also "the people kept changing" within themselves because of the presence and power of the Holy Spirit and the strength of this covenant commitment. These are the reasons it has continued.

4. Why are there only four months of Scriptures listed for Great Experiment groups? The hope is that after four months of reading and applying the Bible as suggested here, the group will have begun to find its way in the Bible. After four months it will be an interesting and formative experience for the group to devise its own plan for getting themselves into the Bible and getting the Bible into themselves.

General Suggestions

It should be clearly understood that *surrender* of one's life to God through Christ is the basic requirement for this spiritual discipline to be most effective. Unless one feels a need to surrender and does so, the Great Experiment will largely miss its mark.

The presentation and interpretation of the challenge of the Great Experiment should be done in the spirit of love. Every person will not respond. Our freedom to decide is precious in the sight of God and we must honor that freedom for others in the spirit of love.

We say, *"Do not deviate in any way* from the program as it is laid out." Here is our reasoning. These are five independent and essential steps in becoming aware of God's transforming power in one's life. We feel they will be helpful if practiced independently, but we know from experience that there is a cumulative value in putting them all together. They add to each other, they supplement each other, and like laminated wood, together they become many times more than five times stronger than when practiced separately. Our practice then has been to follow this entire program *exactly* as it came.

The challenge should be given to every adult and youth alike. All should be invited to accept it within a reasonable time. When the preannounced deadline arrives, the group should be closed for the month. Anyone who becomes interested after the group is closed will be invited to join the next group.

Each group and each individual should be prepared for the "mountaintop experience." This "wonderful feeling" comes when a person experiences conversion. Almost inevitably, it is followed by a "feeling" that is just the opposite of the "mountaintop experience." These high and low moments are natural and are to be expected. They will remind us that our surrender to God through Christ has been made because we love God—and not just for the "good feeling" we get! Surrender is an act of the will and not always an emotional experience.

Commitment Form

WANTED
TEN BRAVE CHRISTIANS
WHO FOR ONE MONTH WILL

1. Meet once each week to pray together.
2. Give two hours time each week to our church. (Self-surrender)
3. Give God one tenth of earnings during this month. (Self-denial)
4. Spend 5:30 to 6:00 each morning in prayer and meditation. (Self-control)
5. Witness for God their experiences to others.

(Please cut along this line)

I have read the above carefully and fully understand the implications of giving my life to God during the month (designated).

To prepare my life to receive from God the great strength and power available through prayer, I ask to be a member of this prayer group.

_____

Signed

_____

Mailing Address

_____

Telephone No.

Please clip on dotted line above and mail to your group leader.

Morning Prayer
and Meditation Schedule

5:30–5:40   Read Scripture for the day (see schedule). Pray and meditate on this Scripture. Write out in fifty words or less how this passage of Scripture applies to your life.

5:40–5:50   Write out one totally unselfish and unexpected act of kindness or generosity that you will do today. Name the person—then act, during the day, vigorously and with love and compassion. Keep a written record of (1) the reaction of the person toward whom the kindness is extended and (2) the effect of this act on you personally.

5:50–6:00   Write out carefully how you would like to build and develop your life. Go into great detail if you desire. Take your time—be thoughtful and prayerful. One well prayed-out and thought-out sentence per day would be excellent progress.

IMPORTANT SUGGESTIONS

Let each of your prayers petition God for:

1. A sense of divine direction for your life.

2. An understanding of the need of total surrender to God's will.

3. Great strength of mind for the development of self-discipline.

Scripture Readings for the First Four Months

FIRST MONTH

The passages for the first month were carefully selected and arranged in a rhythmic pattern. One passage may challenge, the next may affirm, the next may comfort, and the next may arouse. Together, they provide a unique personal invitation to put God first.

Day 1	2 Chron. 7:14	Day 17	Isa. 59:1–3
2	James 4:16	18	Prov. 28:9–10
3	1 John 1:9	19	Matt. 8:24–27
4	John 15:6–7	20	John 6:47
5	Mark 11:24	21	Eccles. 8:1–8
6	Phil. 4:6	22	Ps. 55:22
7	1 John 5:14	23	John 14:27
8	Jer. 29:13	24	Psalms 1:1–8
9	Matt. 6:7–13	25	John 14:1
10	Matt. 18:19	26	Matt. 6:25–33
11	Isa. 65:23–24	27	Ps. 23:1–6
12	Matt. 6:6	28	Mark 12:30
13	Luke 11:9–10	29	Heb. 12:1
14	Isa. 58:9–11	30	John 4:14
15	Ps. 127:1	31	Matt. 5:13–16
16	Ps. 66:18		

SECOND MONTH

When a group continues the disciplines for the second month, the same format continues for the morning devotional time at 5:30. Because the pattern of the three ten-minute segments has been helpful, consider continuing for as long as the group chooses. The group may select its own source of Scripture passages or use the selection listed below. The passages suggested for the second month are on mental and spiritual qualities for building a peaceful, powerful, and productive life.

Day	Qualities	Verse	Day	Qualities	Verse
1	Abiding in Christ	John 15:47	16	Good	Luke 28:50
			17	Gratitude	Col. 2:7
2	Access to God	John 14:6	18	Hope	Rom. 5:5
3	Assurance	Heb. 10:22	19	Self-denial	Matt. 16:24
4	Love	John 13:12	20	Steadfastness	Heb. 12:1–2
5	Compassion	Luke 10:34	21	Virtue	Phil. 4:8
6	Consecration	Exod. 32:29	22	Charity	1 Cor. 13 All Verses
7	Courage	Josh. 1:7	23	Frugality	Gen. 41:35–36
8	Endurance	Matt. 10:32	24	Happiness	Luke 6:23
9	Faith	2 Cor. 5:7	25	Perseverance	1 Cor. 15:58
10	Fidelity	Titus 2:10	26	Purpose	Luke 9:51
11	Forgiveness	Eph. 4:32	27	Reason	Prov. 26:16
12	Fortitude	1 Cor. 15:58	28	Self-control	Prov. 16:32
13	Generosity	Luke 6:38	29	Self-respect	1 Tim. 4:16
14	Giving	Acts 20:35	30	Thrift	1 Cor. 16:2
15	Golden Rule	Matt. 7:12	31	Wisdom	Prov. 8:13

THIRD MONTH

Scripture selections listed for the third month are on two of the most basic tenets of the Christian life: love and prayer. Broadly speaking, we may say that love is the essence of *who you are* and prayer is the essence of *what you do.*

LOVE

Day	1	1 John 4:8	Day	12	Eph. 3:19
	2	Mark 12:32–34		13	John 15:12
	3	1 Tim. 6:10–12		14	1 John 4:7
	4	Prov. 10–12		15	Deut. 6:5–7
	5	Matt. 5:46–47		16	Mic. 6:8
	6	1 John 2:15		17	1 John 4:10
	7	1 John 4:18–21		18	Matt. 22:37–40
	8	Rom. 10:18		19	John 14:15
	9	1 John 5:14–15		20	John 14:18
	10	John 15:17			
	11	Rom. 8:35–39			

PRAYER

Day	21	Phi. 4:6	Day	27	Isa. 65:23–24
	22	Jer. 29:18		28	Isa. 58:9
	23	John 9:81		29	Jer. 33:8
	24	James 5:16		30	1 Kings 8:11–14
	25	1 John 8:22		31	
	26	John 15:6–7			

FOURTH MONTH

The Book of Acts tells of the beginning of the church of Jesus Christ. It tells of the people, the problems, the power, and the promise of the church.

The church will become *first* for the person who *puts God first*. As we consecutively and consistently read the story of the church's beginning in thirty or thirty-one days, it is as if we are "reading it in one sitting." Acts is not only God's story, and the church's story—it is our story.

Acts in Thirty Days

*(Good News for Modern Man)**

Day	Verse	Subject	Day	Verse	Subject
1	1:1–1:26	Dear Theophilus	15	13:1–13:52	Barnabas and Saul
2	2:1–2:47	The Coming of the Holy Spirit			Chosen and Sent
3	3:1–4:22	The Lame Man Healed	16	14:1–14:28	In Iconium
			17	15:1–15:35	The Meeting at Jerusalem
4	4:23–4:37	The Believers Pray for Boldness	18	15:36–16:10	Paul and Barnabas Separate
5	5:1–5:42	Ananias and Sapphira	19	16:11–16:40	In Philippi: The Conversion of Lydia
6	6:1–6:7	The Seven Helpers	20	17:1–17:34	In Thessalonica
7	6:8–7:53	The Arrest of Stephen	21	18:1–18:23	In Corinth
			22	18:24–19:20	Apollos in Ephesus and Corinth
8	7:54–7:60	The Stoning of Stephen	23	19:21–20:6	The Riot in Ephesus
9	8:1–8:40	Saul Persecutes the Church	24	20:7–21:16	Paul's Last Visit in Troas
10	9:1–9:31	The Conversion of Saul	25	21:17–23:11	Paul Visits James
			26	23:12–24:27	The Plot against Paul's Life
11	9:32–10:33	Peter in Lydda and Joppa	27	25:1–26:32	Paul Appeals to the Emperor
12	10:34–10:48	Peter's Speech			
13	11:1–11:30	Peter's Report to the Church at Jerusalem	28	27:1–27:44	Paul Sails for Rome
			29	28:1–28:15	In Malta
14	12:1–12:25	More Persecution	30	28:16–28:31	In Rome

**Good News for Modern Man* is *Today's English Version of The New Testament*, and may be ordered from the American Bible Society, New York.

Self Evaluation

(Look back over your notes for precise details in making your personal evaluation at the end of the first month. This will help you determine whether you have been fair to yourself and to the experiment.)

___YES ___NO   I have followed exactly the half-hour schedule.

_____   I have failed to keep my 5:30 A.M. appointment how many mornings?

_____   I have missed doing the experiment how many days?

___YES ___NO   I have accomplished 3/4 of my good deeds.

___YES ___NO   I have given my 10 percent.

___YES ___NO   I have prayed about my use of the other 90 percent of my income.

___YES ___NO   I have been genuinely open with the group.

___YES ___NO   I am gaining insight into my life through the daily Scriptures.

___YES ___NO   I look for opportunities to talk to people about God.

_____   How many days has it been since I talked with someone specifically about God?

_____   How many hours am I behind in my "two hours a week"?

_____   How many meetings have I missed?

___YES ___NO   Have I surrendered my life to God?

Following your thoughtful and candid evaluation, strike through the phrases of the prayer which *do not* apply to you.

O God, as I come to the close of the Great Experiment, I [feel great] [am sorry] about my faithfulness to you. I have [sincerely] [half-heartedly] tried to put you first in my life. I have [surrendered] [drawn closer] to Jesus Christ as my Savior and Lord. Right now I commit myself to you completely [for the first time] [again]. And before this day is over, I will tell [one person] [two or more persons] of my new commitment. Amen.

_____

Signed

_____

Date

ORDER FORM

For additional copies of this book and/or *The Wesley Experience—Surrendering to the Spirit* please contact:

General Commission on United Methodist Men
PO Box 340006
Nashville TN 37203-0006
Telephone 615-340-7145   Fax 615-340-1770
bgardner@gcumm.org

	A Life That Really Matters (book)	The Wesley Experience (Journal)	Both resources together
Single issue price	$9.95	$5.95	$15 per set
10 or more	$7.50	$4.50	$11 per set

All prices plus shipping and handling charges

Name _____

Address _____

City, State _____

Zip _____

Phone _____

E-mail _____